Framework™
User's Handbook

by
Weber Systems Inc. Staff

CC

CENTURY COMMUNICATIONS
LONDON

First published in Great Britain in 1985 by
Century Communications Ltd,
Portland House,
12–13 Greek Street,
London, W1V 5LE.

Century Communications Ltd. is part
of the Century Hutchinson Group

ISBN 07126 0603 3

Printed and bound in Great Britain by
Butler & Tanner Ltd, Frome and London

Contents

Preface

Framework is an integrated software package from Ashton-Tate. It combines five applications into a single personal computer program:

Data Base Management
Spreadsheet
Word Processing
Graphics
Telecommunications

Framework applies the power of the personal computer to the information management tasks that are prevalent in virtually all professional environments. By combining these software tools into one system, Framework allows you to perform data management tasks with a new level of speed and efficiency. For example, while data is calculated on the spreadsheet, a corresponding memo can be prepared simultaneously in the word processing environment. The results of the spreadsheet can then be displayed and printed graphically in different forms. Each of these individual applications can then be combined into a single report which can be transmitted electronically using the Mite telecommunications program. All of this can be accomplished within the Framework environment using a common set of commands to control the process.

The **Framework User's Handbook** is a concise and practical guide to the Framework program. The book was designed for the busy professional who needs to quickly learn how to apply Framework to everyday information management problems. Although it is not a replacement for the extensive documentation provided by Ashton-Tate, we believe this book will allow the average user to proficiently operate Framework in the shortest possible time.

Beginning with the basics, such as installation and program start up, the **Framework User's Handbook** guides the user through each of the five program modules. Along the way, user tips are presented to help you adapt to the Framework environment. Although this book is not meant as a tutorial on the FRED programming language, chapter 9 introduces some basic principles of this new spreadsheet programming language.

1

Introduction

What Does Framework Do?

Framework is an integrated software system designed to process many kinds of information within one program. The key word here is "integrated." Without integration, operating a computer can sometimes be an awkward, cumbersome process.

For instance, if you were using a word processor and wanted to include the contents of a spreadsheet, it would be difficult to switch from one to the other with non-integrated software packages. You would have to first save the document and close the word processing program. Then you would have to load the spreadsheet program, create the spreadsheet, store the spreadsheet as a disk file and close the spreadsheet program. Finally, you would have to load the word processing program, copy the spreadsheet file into the word processing program and edit it before the final printing.

Framework provides a system of handling word processing, spreadsheets, data base, graphics and communications, all within one program. It does so using structures known as frames, which are used to store elements of information. Each **frame** is designated as either a word frame, a spreadsheet frame, a data base frame, or as a frame to hold other frames. These frames can be organized with a flexibility that allows the user to design his or her own system of information handling.

Outlining is another of Framework's useful features. An outline allows the Framework user to assemble a number of diverse frames into a single document. For example, suppose you were preparing a long report. When you create the outline using Framework's outlining feature, you automatically generate the corresponding word processor frames. You can compose the report in a sequential fashion or you can work in whichever portion (or frame) you choose. The outline will keep the report organized, even if you later add or delete outline entries.

Outlining can be used in many other ways as a productivity aid. Outlining will be discussed in more detail in chapter 3.

Finally Framework even includes its own built-in programming language, FRED, which will be discussed in chapter 9.

How To Use This Handbook

This handbook is designed to provide the user with a concise yet thorough tutorial on Framework. Each section of the book demonstrates the use of an important Framework feature by presenting an example with an accompanying step-by-step explanation.

A brief summary of assumptions is presented at the beginning of each new section. Also, the reader is directed to the next important section provided he is already familiar with the material in the current section.

Experienced software users should find it easy to advance through this book without having to search through material that is already familiar.

The majority of this book has been produced with a type style known as Times Roman. We are however using a second type style named **Megaron**, to denote information* which is to be typed into the computer by the Framework user as well as information which is displayed on the video screen by Framework or DOS.

We recommend that you actually work with Framework as you read this book. By entering the information denoted in **Megaron**, you'll be able to gain valuable hands-on experience with Framework as you read this book.

Equipment Requirements

Framework will operate on the IBM PC, PC XT, and compatibles running PC-DOS or MS-DOS (version 2 or later). The minimum memory requirements are 256K of RAM and two disk drives (either two floppy diskettes or one floppy diskette and one hard disk). The minimum memory requirements for installing the communications module is 384K. Additional memory will allow more spreadsheet cells and more data base records.

---

* Keys which are to be pressed will also be indicated in Megaron. They will be presented in Times Roman when they appear as part of the text.

Disk Configuration

If your system includes two floppy disk drives and you are using Framework for the first time, you may advance to chapter 2 "Starting a Framework Worksession." Framework is ready to run on your system and can be used without any modification. Later when you wish to know more about,

- Booting the system with the Framework disk
- Accessing DOS without changing diskettes
- Changing defaults
- Installation for telecommunications
- Installing Framework Drivers

you may wish to return to this section.

BOOTING THE SYSTEM WITH THE FRAMEWORK DISK

You can start Framework after DOS has been booted by inserting the Framework System Disk 1 in drive (A:) and typing FW [RET]. The inconvenience of having to boot DOS with the DOS system disk prior to loading Framework can be avoided by copying enough of the DOS system disk to the Framework disk to allow DOS to load itself from the Framework disk. To accomplish this:

1. Boot the system, that is start the system with the DOS system disk.
2. Keep the DOS system disk in drive A: and insert the Framework System Disk 1 in drive B:.
3. Type SYS B: [RET]

The expression [RET] is used to indicate that you should press the RETURN key. Now to load Framework with the Framework System Disk 1, insert the disk in drive A: and turn on the computer. Framework will be booted, but you will still need to swap to System Disk 2 before you can accept the licensing agreement.

COPYING DOS TO THE FRAMEWORK DISK

One of Framework's handiest features is its ability to move from data processing to word processing without exiting the system. Sometimes it is necessary to switch to the disk operating system during a Framework work session. This would be inconvenient if you had to exit Framework for a simple DOS operation and then return by reloading Framework.

You can access DOS within Framework, but only if DOS is available. When operating Framework with two drives, System Disk #2 will always be in drive A: and your work disk will be in drive B:. To make DOS accessible, you must copy the operating system to the Framework System Disk #2.

To copy the DOS system to the Framework System Disk #2:

1. Insert the DOS system diskette in drive A: and the Framework System Disk #2 in drive B:
2. Type COPY COMMAND.COM B: [RET]

The DOS system is now copied to the Framework disk allowing you to switch freely from Framework to DOS during a Framework work session.

HARD DISK INSTALLATION

Hard disk installation is accomplished by copying the Framework files to the hard disk. This procedure is virtually automatic when you follow the simple steps outlined here. After this installation, the system will still have to "see" System Disk 1 each time you start Framework, but after the initial "look," no further reference to the Framework diskette will be necessary.

Before you install Framework on the hard disk, you should decide if you want to create a sub-directory to hold all of the Framework files (over 40 files involved). The following procedure assumes that the root directory is C: and that you wish to create a sub-directory for Framework which we will call FRAME. (*See* "Tree Structured Directories" in your DOS reference manual.)

Follow these steps:

1. Boot the system; respond to the DATE and TIME prompts to display the system prompt C>.
2. Create the new directory by typing MD\FRAME [RET].
3. Change directories by typing CD\FRAME [RET]. The system prompt C> should be displayed.
4. Insert the Framework Utilities Disk into drive A: and type A:install [RET] to begin the install sequence.

First you will be asked to choose and enter a command. Then you will be asked to swap diskettes a few times while the program copies the Framework files to the hard disk. Finally the system prompt will appear indicating that installation has been completed.

After the hard disk has been installed, all installation files reside on the hard disk. Therefore, installation of the screen driver, the printer driver, and telecommunications may be accomplished from the hard disk.

Framework can now be started from the hard disk by typing FW [RET] when the system prompt is displayed. It is important to remember that you must be operating from the sub-directory named FRAME. The simple way to do this after the system has been booted is to type CD\FRAME [RET], just as you did in step 3 above. If you plan to use Framework almost exclusively, you may want to use a batch file to instruct your system to load Framework on startup (*See also* "Batch Processing," and "AUTOEXEC.BAT" file in your DOS reference manual).

The commands to create a batch file to start Framework from the hard disk root directory are listed below:

```
COPY CON:FW.BAT [RET]
PATH C:\FRAME [RET]
PAUSE INSERT FRAMEWORK SYSTEM DISK 1 IN DRIVE A: [RET]
ECHO OFF [RET]
CLS [RET]
CD\FRAME [RET]
FW [RET]
[F6] [RET]
```

The first command, COPY CON:, instructs DOS to copy from the console device into FW.BAT. The next five commands are the contents of the batch file, and the last command (Function key 6) ends the batch file and ends the use of the console as the input device. The PATH command instructs DOS to look for .EXE files in the FRAME sub-directory if they cannot be found in the current directory. After this batch file is created, Framework can be started from the root directory by typing FW [RET].

If you want the system to load Framework automatically when the sytem is booted, create a new AUTOEXEC.BAT file with these commands:

```
COPY CON:AUTOEXEC.BAT [RET]
DATE [RET]
TIME [RET]
PATH C:\FRAME [RET]
PAUSE INSERT FRAMEWORK SYSTEM DISK 1 IN DRIVE A: [RET]
ECHO OFF [RET]
CLS [RET]
CD\FRAME [RET]
FW [RET]
[F6] [RET]
```

There is only one AUTOEXEC.BAT file and it is read when the system is booted. The DATE and TIME commands are necessary to enter the system date and time. As indicated before, it is still necessary to insert the Framework System Disk 1 in drive A when starting Framework; otherwise you will experience an "unauthorized copy" error.

After you have installed Framework on the hard disk, you may skip to the next chapter, "Starting A Worksession", if the following sections are not of immediate interest.

Installing Telecommunications

TWO DISK DRIVES

CAUTION — Installing Framework for telecommunications will reset the file CONFIG.FW on System Disk 2 to its original defaults.

To install Framework for telecommunications, follow these steps:

1. Boot the system and be certain that the system prompt A> is displayed.
2. With the Framework System Disk 1 in drive A:, type INSTCOMM [RET] to start the program that will install Framework for telecommunications.

After Framework has been installed for telecommunications, a frame labeled UTIL will be displayed on the desktop each time that Framework is started. If you are not using telecommunications during any particular session, then this frame may be deleted to provide the maximum memory available.

Telecommunications may be deinstalled by renaming the file FWT.EXE to FW.EXE on Framework System Disk 1.

HARD DISK

CAUTION — Installing Framework for telecommunications will reset the file CONFIG.FW on System Disk 2 to its original defaults.

To install Framework for telecommunications, follow these steps:

1. Boot the system and be certain that the system prompt C> is displayed. This assumes that Framework has already been installed for the hard disk.
2. With the Framework System Disk 1 in drive A:, type INSTCOMM [RET] to start a program that will install Framework for telecommunications.

After Framework is installed for telecommunications, a frame labeled UTIL will be displayed on the desktop every time Framework is started. If you are not using telecommunications during any particular session, then this frame may be deleted to provide the maximum memory available.

Telecommunications may be deinstalled by renaming the file FWT.EXE to FW.EXE on Framework System Disk 1.

CONFIGURING FRAMEWORK

Framework generally does not have to be reconfigured to run efficiently for most uses. However, once you have become an expert at using Framework, you may wish to establish more efficient default settings for your particular application. A listing of the default settings and a brief description of each is outlined below.

To change any of these default settings, it is necessary to start Framework and open the disk file CONFIG.FW. Follow the instructions given in this file to change the settings. You must then restart Framework to make the new settings effective.

FRAMEWORK CONFIGURATION DEFAULT SETTINGS

KEEP_OVERLAY   **#FALSE**

If your computer contains over 320K of memory, change the setting above to #TRUE to improve Framework's speed.

OVERLAY_SIZE   **16**

This option sets the size of Framework's overlay buffer.

DEFAULT_DRIVE   **0**

This option sets the default drive.

DISK_FRAME_WIDTH   **27**

DISK_FRAME_HEIGHT   **9**

These two options set the size of the open disk drive frames.

DOCUMENT_CREATE_WIDTH   **70**

DOCUMENT_CREATE_HEIGHT   **11**

GRAPH_CREATE_WIDTH   **55**

GRAPH_CREATE_HEIGHT   **14**

These four options set the initial size of documents and graphs created on the desktop (not within another frame).

SS_COLUMN_WIDTH   **9**

This option sets the default size of spreadsheet columns and database fields.

SS_WIDTH   **14**

SS_HEIGHT   **14**

These two options set defaults for the Create menu's Width (#Cols/Fields) and Height (#Rows/Records) commands.

WORD_LEFTMARGIN	0
WORD_RIGHTMARGIN	65
WORD_PARAGRAPH_INDENT	0
WORD_TABSIZE	8

These four options set defaults for the last group of Words menu commands.

PRINTER1	"LPT1"
PRINTER2	"LPT2"
PLOTTER	"COM1"

The Print menu enables you to choose a First Printer, a Second Printer, or a Plotter as the destination of a printout. These three options set the ports which receive the output.

PRINTER1_SPEED	5
PRINTER2_SPEED	5

These two options set the amount of data Framework sends to a printer while you are in fact working in Framework.

WINDOW_ORPHAN_TOLERANCE   3

In the printing of text, a "widow" is the part of a paragraph carried to the next page. An "orphan" is the part that is left on the previous page. This option sets the minimum number of lines allowed stranded as a widow or orphan when a paragraph is broken.

TOP_MARGIN	6
BOTTOM_MARGIN	6
PAGE_OFFSET	10
LINE_LENGTH	65
PAGE_LENGTH	66
SPACING	1

This group of options sets defaults for printing functions entered in the border of frames.

MAX_WHILE	2048

This option sets the maximum number of times FRED will execute a @while loop.

CURRENCY_SYMBOL	@DOLLAR
CURRENCY_UNITS	@THOUSANDS
CURRENCY_POSITION	#BEFORE

These three options set the default currency symbol, units, and symbol position for numbers formatted by the Currency command in the Numbers menu.

DOS_ACCESS	2000

This option sets the number of characters a DOS Access frame returns during a DOS Access session. Once this number is reached, Framework erases characters from the beginning of the frame to make room for new characters.

UTIL_NAME	"Telecommunications"

This option sets the name of the second to the last command in the Disk menu. The setting must be in "double quotes."

ZOOMDELAY   **1**

This option sets the number of seconds Framework takes to "zoom" open or "zoom" close frames or disk drives.

USE_87   **#TRUE**

If this setting is #TRUE, the 8087 math chip is used if installed. If #FALSE, the 8087 chip is not used.

SERIALNUMBER   **0**

This option controls access to Framework formulas.

INSTALLING FRAMEWORK DRIVERS

Drivers are sub-programs supplied with Framework that allow it to operate with your specific hardware. The two kinds of drivers supplied with Framework are printer and screen drivers. To install these drivers, follow these steps:

1. Insert the Framework Utility Disk into drive A:.
2. Type A: INSTALL if you have two disk drives, or just INSTALL if you have already installed Framework on your hard disk.

These steps start Framework's installation sequence which provides the options of installing screen, printer, or plotter drivers (and the option of installing Framework on a hard disk).

2

Starting a Framework Worksession

Starting Framework

If you are starting Framework for the very first time on your system, we advise that you return to chapter 1 and read the sections on Equipment Requirements and Disk Configuration. We especially emphasize this if you have a hard disk system. Readers with dual floppy drive systems may proceed without reading chapter 1. Eventually you should read chapter 1 as this will enable you to use your system more effectively.

In the following procedures, we assume that the operator is familiar with the computer's resident disk operating system (DOS). DOS is the file management system supplied with your computer. If you have questions about DOS, refer to your computer's Guide to Operations or DOS reference manual.

Starting Framework With Two Disk Drives

To start Framework with two disk drives, follow these steps:

1. Boot the system, that is start the system with the DOS system disk. You may start the system with Framework System Disk 1 if you have transferred the system as outlined in chapter 1 (*See* chapter 1, "Booting the System with the Framework Disk").

2. With the system prompt A> displayed, insert the Framework System Disk 1 into drive A: and type FW [RET]. The expression [RET] is used to indicate that you should press the Return key.

3. When the Framework opening screen display appears followed by the licensing agreement, swap the Framework System Disk 2 with the System Disk 1 in drive A: and press [RET]. The Framework Desktop will appear (*See* figure 2.1).

Starting Framework With a Hard Disk

To start Framework with a hard disk drive, follow these steps: (It is assumed that Framework has been installed on the hard disk.)

1. Boot the system.

2. With the system prompt C: displayed, insert the Framework System disk 1 in drive A: and type FW. Be sure that you are in the right directory if you have created a special directory for Framework.

3. When the Framework opening screen display appears followed by the licensing agreement, press [RET]. The Framework Desktop will appear (*See* figure 2.1).

Figure 2.1 depicts the Framework desktop screen. We will explain the desktop's features as the need arises. In the next section, we explain the procedure for creating and saving (on disk) a word processing file.

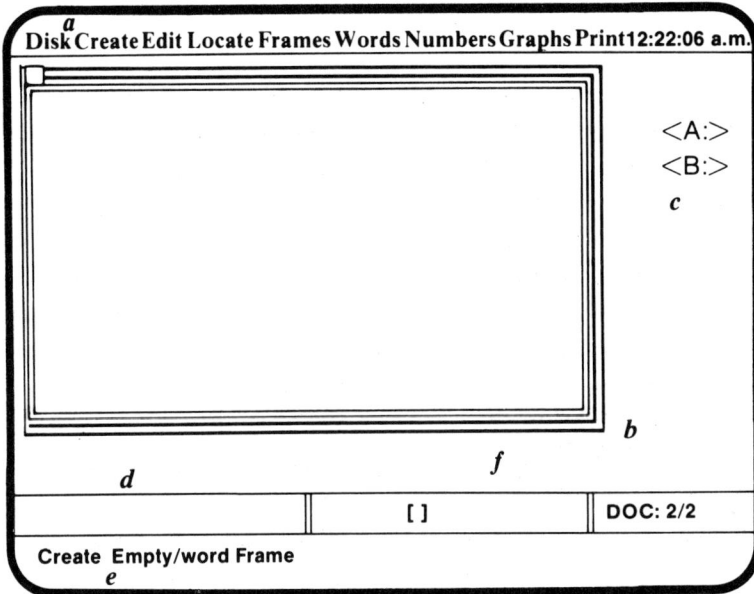

Figure 2.1. The Framework desktop screen.

a) menu bar   b) frame   c) disk drive   d) status panel   e) message area
f) desktop

Creating a File

Before you can save a file, you must have a disk available for storage. For systems with two floppy disk drives, the Framework System Disk #2 should be present in drive A: and a formatted work disk in drive B:. For hard disk systems the work disk should reside in drive A: with Framework installed on drive C: (the hard disk).

DISPLAY DISK DIRECTORIES

On the right-hand side of the desktop display, you will see the two disk drive symbols displayed as follows:

<A:>
<B:>

The cursor will be flashing on one of these, and if you press [RET] at this time a frame will appear on the desktop. Within that frame you will see a list of files displayed. Press [RET] again and the frame with the list of files disappears.

To view the other drive's display, press one of the arrow keys on the numeric keypad on the right side of the keyboard. Pressing any one of the cursor movement keys repeatedly will alternate the cursor between the two drives. After selecting the desired drive, press the [RET] key to display the frame with the list of files on that drive.

Notice that you can display both drives on the desktop at the same time. For two-drive systems, drive A: will contain a display of files from System Disk #2, and drive B: will display your work disk files. For hard drive systems, drive A: displays the work disk files, and drive C: displays the hard disk files.

Since we are going to create some new files for practice and store them on the work disk, close both of the displays by moving the cursor to each displayed frame and pressing [RET].

ACCESSING THE CREATE PULLDOWN MENU

Now to create a new file, press [INS]. A list of **pulldown menus** are displayed at the top of your screen. These menus are chosen by pressing the [INS] key. The expression [INS] is used to indicate that you should press the 'Insert' key which is located just below the numeric keypad next to the [DEL] key.

When you press [INS], you are instructing Framework to display one of these pulldown menus.

The first time you press [INS] after loading Framework, the Create menu will appear as shown in figure 2.2. If another menu is displayed, press the cursor movement keys (left or right on the numeric keypad) until the Create Menu is displayed.

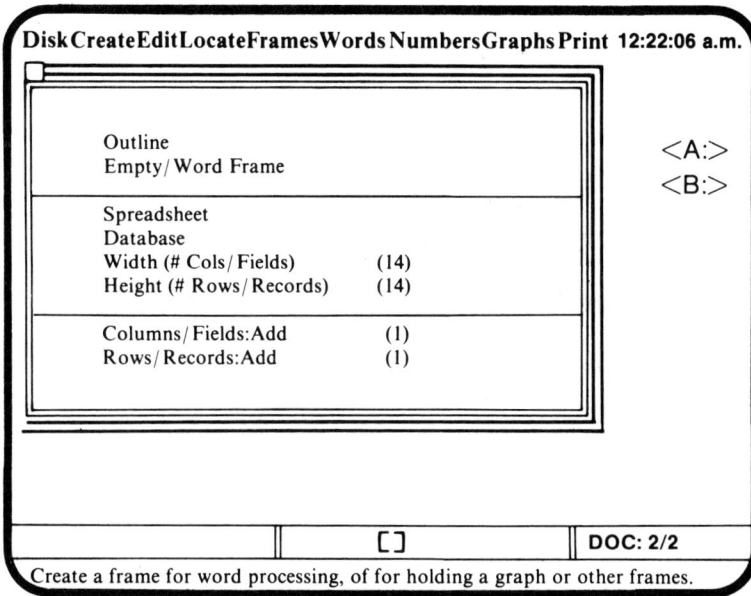

```
Disk Create Edit Locate Frames Words Numbers Graphs Print   12:22:06 a.m.

          Outline                                              <A:>
          Empty/Word Frame                                     <B:>

          Spreadsheet
          Database
          Width (# Cols/Fields)        (14)
          Height (# Rows/Records)      (14)

          Columns/Fields:Add           (1)
          Rows/Records:Add             (1)




                                 [ ]              DOC: 2/2
  Create a frame for word processing, of for holding a graph or other frames.
```

Figure 2.2.   Framework desktop with Create Menu displayed.

Notice that the highlight is positioned on Empty/Word Frame. You can select other kinds of frames by moving the highlight up or down with the cursor movement keys. The other choices are Outline, Spreadsheet, or Database. You can practice moving the highlight now if you wish, but return it to Empty/Word Frame.

Now to create an empty word processing frame, press [RET]. A large empty frame will be displayed on the desktop with the cursor flashing in its left-hand border. The frame should be labeled so that it can be recognized later when you store it on disk. Call it Word1 (for word processing frame number 1).

LABEL THE FRAME

To **label** the frame, type the label, Word1, and press [RET]. Notice as you type that the letters immediately appear on the frame border and in the message area at the bottom of the screen. If you make a mistake or if you wish to change the label at any time, move the cursor to the frame border, retype the label and press [RET].

ENTERING TEXT

Before typing a document, you must move the cursor into the contents of the frame by pressing the gray [+] or [DOWN-LEVEL] key located just to the right of the numeric keypad. The gray [-] or [UPLEVEL] key, which is located just above the gray [+] key, moves the cursor back to the border of the frame.

Once the cursor has been moved into the frame with the [DOWNLEVEL] key, type the following:

> This is a newly created word processing frame. To
> type in this frame, simply press the [DOWNLEVEL]
> key (gray plus) and start typing. There is a com-
> plete chapter in this book describing word
> processing with Framework. To escape from this
> frame, return to the border by pressing the
> [UPLEVEL] key (gray minus).

Return to the border of the frame by pressing the [UPLEVEL] key. Now press [RET] to close the frame and clear the desktop.

CLOSING A FRAME IN ITS TRAY

When you **closed** the frame, you stored the frame in a **tray**. Trays are located in the lower right-hand corner of the screen. Each time a tray is closed, the corresponding frame zooms down to the size of a tray and is stacked neatly in this corner. To recall a frame that has been stored in a tray, simply use the cursor movement keys to select the tray desired and press [RET]. Since there is only one tray available now, press [RET] to reopen the frame labeled "Word1". Now press [RET] to again store the frame in its tray.

It is important to understand that closing a frame into its tray does **not** create a permanent copy of the frame on disk. The tray is only a convenient space for storage in memory. After we create another frame, we will explain how to save frames on disk.

Follow these steps to create another word processing frame labeled "Word2":

1. Press [INS] to display a pulldown menu.
2. Use the cursor movement keys (left or right) to choose the Create menu.
3. Use the cursor movement keys (up or down) to highlight Empty/Word Frame.
4. Press [RET] to create the empty word frame.
5. Type Word2 [RET] to label the newly created frame.
6. Press [DOWNLEVEL] to enter the word frame and type the following:

   This is the second word processing frame created for practice.
7. Press [UPLEVEL] to return to the border of the frame.
8. Press [RET] to store the frame in its tray.

This completes the section on starting Framework. In this section we have covered the following:

1. Starting Framework.
2. Displaying disk files.
3. Selecting pulldown menus.
4. Creating word processing frames.
5. Storing frames in trays.

Now that we have two files created and stored neatly in their trays, it is time to save them on disk.

Saving Frames On Disk

To save a frame during program operation, simply press [CTRL] [RET]. This is a quick, automatic way to save the entire file and continue without interruption. This procedure can be executed from the border or from inside any frame or subframe.

To save the frames Word1 and Word2 on your work disk, follow these steps:

1. Use the cursor movement keys to select the tray that you wish to save, say Word1.
2. Press [INS] to display a pulldown menu.
3. Use the cursor movement keys (right or left) to choose the Disk pulldown menu.
4. Use the cursor movement keys (up or down) to move the highlight to Save and Continue.
5. Press [RET] to save the file Word1.
6. Repeat steps 1 to 5 above for the frame Word2.

There is a shortcut available when saving multiple frames which involves the use of F6, the Extend Select key. F6 is one of the 10 program function keys located on the left-hand side of the keyboard.

To save more than one file at a time, follow this procedure:

1. Move the cursor to one of the frames that you wish to save on disk.
2. Press [F6 Extend Select].
3. Use the cursor movement keys to highlight other frames that you wish to save.
4. Type [CTRL] D S to save all of the frames that were highlighted in step 3. When the [CTRL] key is specified, hold the [CTRL] key down while pressing the next key indicated. (In this case hold the [CTRL] key down while pressing "D".)

Finally note that although the three following choices in the Disk pulldown menu are similar, there are important differences between these:

SAVE AND CONTINUE Save (on disk) the frame or frames selected and continue processing.

PUT AWAY Save (on disk) the frame or frames selected and remove the trays from the desktop.

CLEAN UP DESKTOP Move all of the displayed frames into their trays, but **do not** save them on disk.

MENU SELECTION SHORTCUTS

There are more efficient ways to save frames than the procedure just outlined. For instance you can use the shorthand method for choosing the Disk menu by using the [CTRL] key.

Notice that no two menu names begin with the same letter. If you hold down the [CTRL] key while pressing the first letter of the menu you wish to choose, then that menu will be displayed. Items within the menu can also be selected by typing the first letter of the desired item.

Using this shorthand method, you can save a frame with the following procedure:

1. Use the cursor keys to select the frame you wish to save.
2. Type [CTRL] D S to save the file.

The following rules apply to menu selection shortcuts:

1. You may choose a menu by holding down the [CTRL] key while typing the first letter of the name of the desired menu. To choose the Disk menu for example, type:

[CTRL] D

2. You may select a specific menu item by typing the first letter of the menu item (either with or without the [CTRL] key). For example to save a file, position the cursor on or within the desired frame border and type:

[CTRL] D S

3. Pressing [INS] when a menu is already displayed has the same effect as pressing [RET]. Therefore, if your last menu operation was "Saving a File," then pressing [INS] will display the Disk menu, and the highlight will be positioned at Save and Continue. If you press [INS] again, the current file will be saved. For example to save a file and continue (when this is a repeat of your last menu operation), type:

[INS][INS]

4. A special purpose shortcut for saving the current file on disk is simply:

[CTRL][RET]

This will save the current file on the current drive or on the drive from which it was originally copied.

This completes our discussion on saving frames on disk. Continue with the next section to learn how to retrieve a file from disk.

Retrieving A File

In this section we assume that you have familiarized yourself with the techniques described in the previous section, namely starting the system, starting Framework, and accessing the Framework desktop.

We will demonstrate the process of retrieving a file by recalling Word1 and Word2 which were created in the previous section and stored on disk. We assume that the work disk contains these files.

We will further assume that your system has two floppy disk drives and the system is not on.

To start the sytem and retrieve a file, follow these steps:

1. Boot the system.

2. With the system prompt A> displayed and the Framework System Disk 1 in drive A:, type FW [RET]. The Framework opening screen display should appear followed by the licensing agreement.

3. Remove the Framework System Disk 1, insert Framework System Disk 2 in drive A: and press [RET].The Framework desktop should be displayed. *See* figure 2.1.

4. Insert your work disk containing the files Word1 and Word2.

    On the right-hand side of the desktop display, the two disk drive symbols will be displayed as follows:

    <A:>
    <B:>

    The cursor will be flashing on one of these disk drive symbols.

5. Select the drive containing your work disk by using the cursor movement keys or the arrow keys.

6. When the cursor is flashing on the drive containing the work disk, press [RET]. A frame should be displayed containing the directory of files from the work disk. *See* figure 2.3.

7. Press the [DOWNLEVEL] key to move the cursor into the frame so that a file can be selected. This is the gray [+] key just to the right of the numeric keypad. One of the files listed in the frame should be highlighted in reverse image.

8. Select the file, Word1, by moving the highlight with the cursor movement keys to that file and pressing [RET]. Word1 will be read into memory from the work disk, and it will be stored in a tray in the lower right-hand corner of the desktop, just above the status panel. *See* figure 2.3.

9. To display Word1's contents, press the [RET] key. A frame containing the contents of the file will be displayed on the desktop.

Note that sometimes when a file is read into memory as in step 8, it is immediately displayed as well as stored in its tray. This depends on the procedure used when the file was stored on disk. If the file was being displayed when it was stored on disk, it will be immediately displayed when retrieved from disk. If the file was saved from its tray, then it will return to its tray when retrieved from disk.

10. You can modify this file by using [DOWNLEVEL] to move the cursor into the body of the text.

You have just completed the procedure for starting Framework and retrieving an existing file from your work disk. The file is displayed on the desktop where it can be modified.

Now let's retrieve another file from your work disk, Word2. To do so, we will first close the frame containing Word1. We will then return to the frame containing the list of files from the work disk and select Word2.

To retrieve Word2, follow these steps:

1. Return the cursor to the border of the frame containing the file Word1 by pressing the [UPLEVEL] key. This is the gray [-] located just to the right of the numeric keypad.

2. With the cursor located (and flashing) on the border of the frame Word1, press the [RET] key. This will close the frame in its tray; the cursor will be flashing in the tray.

3. Press the [Scroll Lock] key to return the cursor to the disk files frame. The cursor will return to the last file selected from the last disk menu displayed, in this case WORD1.FW on your work disk in drive B:. The [Scroll Lock] key acts as a toggle to switch from frames to disk or from disk to frames. It is located in the upper right-hand corner of the keyboard.

4. Move the highlight to the file WORD2.FW with the cursor movement keys and select the file by pressing the [RET] key. The file Word2 will be read into memory from your work disk, and it will be stored in a tray in the lower right-hand corner of the desktop just above the status panel.

5. To see the contents of the file Word2 displayed, press the [RET] key. A frame containing the contents of the file will be displayed on the desktop.

6. If you wish to modify this file, you may move the cursor into the frame by pressing the [DOWNLEVEL] key.

Cleaning Up The Desktop

Before we end this Framework session, let's clean up the desktop. The following procedures can be used at any time during a Framework session to clear away all frames from the desktop.

1. Press the [INS] key to display a pulldown menu.

2. Use the cursor movement keys (right or left) to choose the Disk pulldown menu.

3. Use the cursor movement keys (up or down) to highlight Clean Up Desktop.

4. Press [RET] to return each frame to its tray.

The shortcut command which selects Clean Up Desktop is [CTRL]-D C.

Continue to the next section to learn how to exit from Framework as well as how to access DOS within the Framework program.

Exiting Framework

In previous sections you learned how to start Framework, create files, save files, retrieve files and clear the desktop. In this section we will explain how to exit Framework.

Two methods are available for exiting Framework. The first is to exit to DOS within Framework, and the second is to terminate Framework and return to DOS.

First we will outline the steps required to terminate Framework and return to DOS.

To terminate Framework, be sure that you have saved your files on disk and then follow these steps:

1. Press [INS] and use the cursor movement keys to select the Disk pulldown menu.

2. Use the cursor movement keys to highlight QUIT Framework. The following will appear in the message area at the bottom of the screen:

Exit Framework, return to DOS (Work not saved will be lost)

You may change your mind about exiting at this time. If you arrived at this step by accident, press [ESC] to return to the desktop without losing any of your work.

3. Press [RET]. All frames that are open on the desktop will be closed and returned to their trays. The following message will appear in the message area at the bottom of the screen:

Document new or modified: SAVE IT (y/n)?

If you type y, the document(s) will be saved before Framework is terminated. If you press n, the termination sequence will continue without saving the document(s). Either selection will result in the following display:

>>>Do you really want to QUIT Framework (y/n)?<<<

This is your last chance to retrieve any work that has not been saved. If you want to return to the desktop, type n.

4. If you want to terminate Framework, type y. Framework will terminate, and the system prompt A> will be displayed.

EXITING FRAMEWORK SHORTCUT

To exit Framework quickly, follow these steps:

1. With the desktop displayed, press [CTRL] D Q. If you have created a new file or made some changes to an existing file, the following may be displayed in the message area at the bottom of the screen.

Document new or modified: SAVE IT (y/n)?

If you type y, the document(s) will be saved before Framework is terminated. If you press n, the termination sequence will continue without saving the document(s). Either selection will result in the following display:

>>>Do you really want to QUIT Framework   (y/n)?<<<

2. To terminate Framework and return to DOS, type y.

EXIT TO DOS WITHIN FRAMEWORK

It is possible to exit to DOS within Framework. This is convenient, particularly if you need to exit briefly to perform file maintenance or run another program.

There are two prerequisites for accessing DOS within Framework. First you must have the system available on the Framework System Disk #2 (in drive A:). Refer to chapter 1, "Copying DOS to the Framework Disk." Second you must access DOS from within a word frame.

To access DOS within Framework, follow these steps:

1. Press [CTRL] C E to create an empty word frame.
2. Press [CTRL] D D to access DOS. Framework will automatically label the empty frame DOS Access Frame.

There are some limitations to creating empty word frames. For instance, an empty word frame cannot be created inside a word frame that contains text, but an empty word frame can be created inside another empty word frame.

3. After completion of step 2, the DOS prompt will be displayed inside the empty word frame. The whole screen can be used to display the DOS operations by pressing the [F9 ZOOM] key prior to step 2.

   Type EXIT [RET] to return to Framework after you have completed your external programs.

When operating DOS within Framework, all of the displays are saved in the frame created for DOS access up to the limits of the size of the frame. When the frame is filled, Framework erases characters from the beginning of the frame to make room for new characters. The size of this frame is specified (and it can be changed) in the configuration file. *See* "Framework Configuration Default Settings" in chapter 1.

The DOS access frame will be saved on the desktop and must be deleted if you do not wish to save it or have it clutter your desktop. To delete the frame, move the cursor to the frame border or highlight the tray and press [DEL].

This completes the section on exiting Framework. Continue to the next chapter to learn more about the techniques of using Framework.

3

Organizing Your Work

This section is designed to increase your ability to take advantage of Framework's many features. In chapters 1 and 2, you learned how to start Framework, create files, save files, retrieve files, and exit Framework.

In this chapter, you will learn how to use Framework to organize your work. You will see that frames can be changed in size, moved around on the screen, and placed in an outline that provides an arrangement of frames based on priority.

The final two sections of this chapter describe disk operations and printing.

WORKING WITH FRAMES

The frame is the basic element Framework uses to organize your work. A frame holds the information to be processed. There are several different types of frames. Word frames are used for word processing. Spreadsheet frames, data base frames, outline frames, and containing frames (which contain other frames) are also available.

Independent Frames

In this section we will learn some of the operations that can be performed with independent frames. An independent frame is a single frame that is not positioned inside another frame.

CREATE AN EMPTY WORD FRAME

With the desktop empty create an empty word frame with the commands [CTRL] C E.

The empty frame will appear on the desktop, and the cursor will be flashing in the label area of the frame.

LABEL THE FRAME

With the cursor positioned in the label area, type the name of the frame, say TRIAL1. Notice that as you type, the label appears in the label area as well as in the tray located in the lower right-hand corner of the desktop. Complete the label entry by pressing [RET].

If you make a mistake while entering the label, you can correct it by merely retyping. Or if you have not pressed [RET], move the cursor with the cursor movement keys to the incorrect letter(s) and use the delete key to erase these. Then retype the correct letters.

ENTER A FRAME FORMULA

There is a "hidden area" behind the label that may contain a **frame formula**. This formula area can be used to create a heading that will appear on each page of printed output. To enter a frame formula, move the cursor to the border of the frame and press [F2 Edit formula]. Now type the following:

@hc("TRIAL1   FRAME HEADING") [RET]

When you press [RET], the formula is stored "behind" the label, but at least part of the formula can be seen on the left side of the status line at the bottom of the screen. Frame formulas can be used to control printed output. Page numbering can be omitted or changed. Also, page length, margins, headers, and footers can all be controlled with frame formulas. For more information on the use of formulas to control printing, see the section on printing later in this chapter.

DRAG THE FRAME

Frames can be moved on the screen with the Drag key, [F3]. To drag the frame, move the cursor to the border of the frame to be moved and press [F3 Drag]. Then use the cursor movement keys to move the frame to the desired location on the screen. As you use the cursor movement keys, a ghost image of the border of the frame will move so that you can recognize the new location. Press [RET] when this ghost image reaches the desired location.

SIZE THE FRAME

To change the size of a frame, move the cursor to the border of the frame to be sized and press the [F4 Size] key. Then use the cursor movement keys to change the size of the frame. Here again, a ghost image of the frame border will move so that you can recognize the new frame size. Press [RET] to complete the size operation.

ZOOM THE FRAME TO FULL DESKTOP SIZE

You can expand the size of the frame to the full desktop by moving the cursor either to the frame border or inside the frame and pressing [F9 Zoom]. Press [F9 Zoom] again to return the frame to its original size.

If you press the Zoom key with the cursor located on the border of the frame, the frame expands to the full desktop size and the cursor moves into the frame so that text can be entered. When you press the Zoom key again, the frame returns to its original size, but the cursor remains inside the frame. To return the cursor to the frame border, you must press the [UPLEVEL] (gray -) key.

COPY A FRAME

An entire frame can be copied into another containing frame. Before we can demonstrate this, we must create another frame. To create the new frame, press the [INS] key to choose a pulldown menu. Move the pulldown menu selection with the cursor movement keys until the **Create** menu is in view. Move the highlight down to **Empty / Word Frame** with the cursor movement keys, and press [RET] to create the new frame. The new frame should appear on the desktop; label it TRIAL2 and press [RET].

To copy TRIAL1 into TRIAL2, move the cursor to the border of TRIAL1 by pressing the [↑] cursor movement key. Press [F8 Copy] and then move the cursor to the border of the frame labeled TRIAL2 using the [↓] cursor movement key. Use the [DOWNLEVEL] (gray+) key to move the cursor into the frame. Press [RET] to complete the copy. The cursor should be flashing on the border of the new trial frame located inside the frame TRIAL2.

The Copy operation can be used to copy text as well as whole frames. Further information is available on the Copy operation in the chapter on word processing (*see* chapter 4 "Word Processing with Framework").

MOVE A FRAME

The Move operation is identical to the Copy operation except that the original frame is moved rather than copied to the new location. The original frame is erased from its previous location. To demonstrate this, delete the frame TRIAL1 inside the frame TRIAL2. To delete the frame, move the cursor to the frame border and press [DEL].

Now move the cursor to the border of the frame labeled TRIAL1 and press [F7 Move]. Move the cursor with the cursor movement keys to the border of the frame labeled TRIAL2, and then use the [DOWNLEVEL] (gray + key) to move the cursor into the frame. Now press [RET] to complete the move. Note the tray which contains TRIAL1 has moved from the desktop.

The Move operation can be used to copy text as well as whole frames. More information can be found on the Move operation in the chapter on word processing (*see* chapter 4 "Word Processing with Framework").

Outline Frames

In the previous section, we learned many of the operations that can be performed on independent frames. The great power of Framework lies in its ability to handle many frames which may have a different structure but are related.

The outline frame provides for the organization of frames in an outline form. To illustrate its use we will create an outline frame and then label several frames in the outline.

CREATING AN OUTLINE FRAME

Starting with a clean desktop, create an outline frame by using the [CTRL] C O commands.

An empty outline frame will be displayed as shown in figure 3.1. Note that the frame contains an outline of number headings. These numbers indicate the three major sections of the outline. Three subsections appear under each major section in the outline. The symbol " ▶ " in front of the major sections indicates that these sections contain subsections. The (E) following each subsection indicates an empty frame.

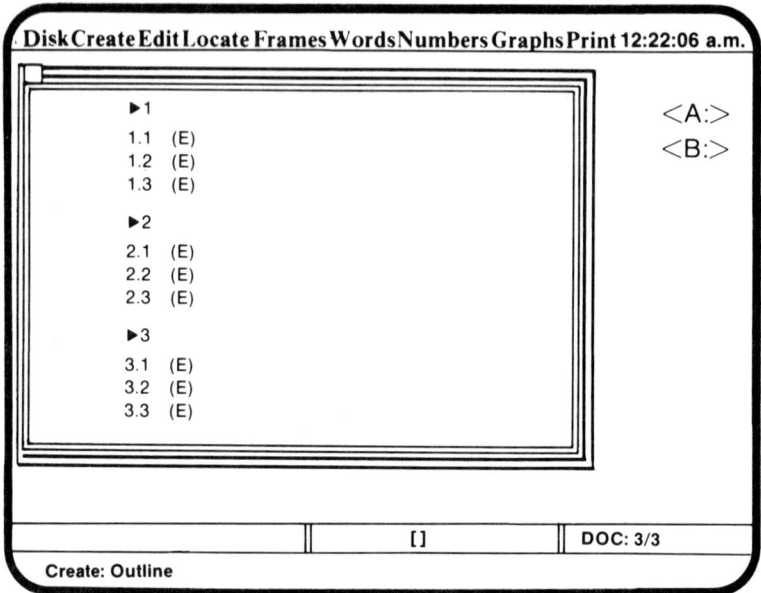

Figure 3.1. Empty outline frame

NAMING SECTIONS OF THE OUTLINE

The following steps illustrate how to add titles to the outline.

1. First label the frame by typing OUTLINE1 [RET].

If you make a typing error while entering the label, just retype the label and press [RET] again. Another method of editing the label is to press the space bar. When the space bar is pressed, the label appears in the message area below the status line on the desktop. Use the cursor movement keys to locate the cursor over the mistake, delete the incorrect characters and retype the correct letters. Press [RET] to end label edit.

2. Use [DOWNLEVEL] (gray+) to move the cursor to the inside of the frame.

The highlight should be positioned on the first major section.

3. Type FINANCIAL and then press [TAB].

FINANCIAL is the name of the first major section. The [TAB] key is located just above the [CTRL] key. Pressing the [TAB] key completes the entry of the section and moves the highlight to the next section (or subsection) in the outline. You could also complete the entry by pressing [RET] followed by the cursor down key, but that would require two keystrokes instead of one.

4. Now name the next three subsections as follows:

Type SALES FIGURES   Press [TAB]
Type P & L   Press [TAB]
Type ACCOUNTING   Press [TAB]

```
┌─────────────────────────────────────────────────────────────┐
│ Disk Create Edit Locate Frames Words Numbers Graphs Print 12:22:06 a.m. │
│  ┌──────────────────────────────────────────┐                │
│  │  ▶1   FINANCIAL                            │                │
│  │  1.1  SALES FIGURES  (E)                   │        <A:>    │
│  │  1.2  P & L  (E)                           │        <B:>    │
│  │  1.3  ACCOUNTING  (E)                      │                │
│  │  ▶2                                        │                │
│  │  2.1  (E)                                  │                │
│  │  2.2  (E)                                  │                │
│  │  2.3  (E)                                  │                │
│  │  ▶3                                        │                │
│  │  3.1  (E)                                  │                │
│  │  3.2  (E)                                  │                │
│  │  3.3  (E)                                  │                │
│  │                                            │                │
│  └──────────────────────────────────────────┘                │
│                            []              DOC: 3/3           │
│  Create: Outline                                              │
└─────────────────────────────────────────────────────────────┘
```

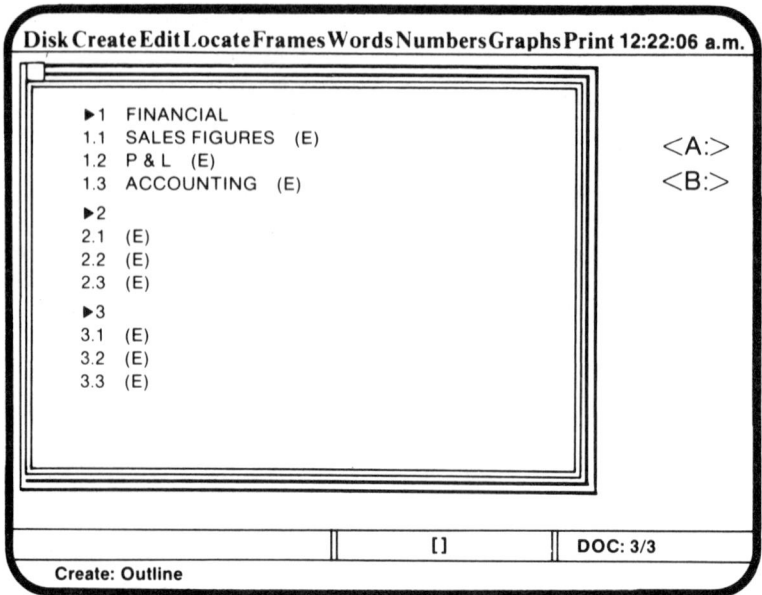

Figure 3.2.   Outline with subsections

This completes the naming of the first major section and its subsections. The outline should now appear as shown in figure 3.2. It is easy to see how the remaining sections could be named using the above procedure. Now let us see how to add additional subsections to the outline.

ADDING SECTIONS AND SUBSECTIONS TO THE OUTLINE

Suppose that you wish to add additional subsections under the accounting subsection. Follow these steps:

1. Move the highlight to the section named ACCOUNT-
   ING and press [CTRL] [DOWNLEVEL].

A new subsection "1.3.1   (E)" will be created under 1.3.

2. Label this subsection PAYABLES and press [RET].

3. With the highlight positioned on PAYABLES, create another subsection "1.3.2 (E)" by choosing the Create menu. When the Create menu appears, move the highlight down to Empty/ Word Frame and press [RET].

A new subsection, 1.3.2, will be created under 1.3.1.

4. Name this subsection RECEIVABLES [RET].

Note that [CTRL][DOWNLEVEL] is used to create the first new subsection, but the create menu is used to create additional subsections or major sections.

When you create a new subsection in an outline, the new subsection appears just under the section highlighted. When you create a new major section in an outline, the new section is inserted immediately after the highlighted section, and all subsequent sections and subsections are renumbered to accommodate the new insertion. The outline should now appear as shown in figure 3.3.

```
Disk Create Edit Locate Frames Words Numbers Graphs Print  12:22:06 a.m.

   ▶1   FINANCIAL
        1.1   SALES FIGURES   (E)                      <A:>
        1.2   P & L   (E)                               <B:>
        ▶1.3  ACCOUNTING
              1.3.1  PAYABLES   (E)
              1.3.2  RECEIVABLES   (E)
   ▶2
        2.1   (E)
        2.2   (E)
        2.3   (E)
   ▶3
        3.1   (E)
        3.2   (E)
        3.3   (E)



                              []              DOC: 3/3
   Create: Outline
```

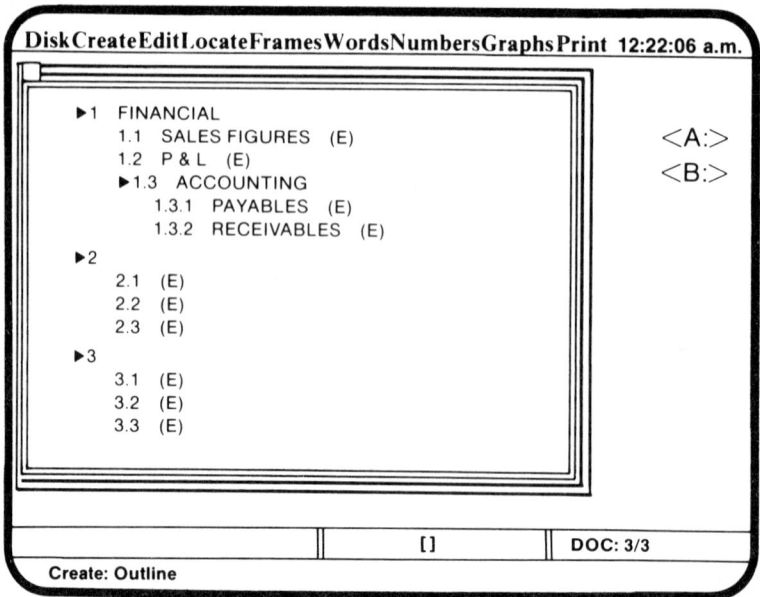

Figure 3.3.   Outline with additional subsections

MOVING SECTIONS AND SUBSECTIONS

Suppose that you now wish to add another subsection before PAYABLES under ACCOUNTING. You must first create the new subsection, which will follow PAYABLES. Then you must move PAYABLES to the second position.

Follow this procedure:

1. With the highlight on PAYABLES, choose the Create menu and select Empty / Word Frame with the highlight.
2. Press [RET] to create the new subsection.
3. Name the new subsection GENERAL LEDGER [RET].
4. Move the highlight to PAYABLES.

5. Press [F7 Move] and then move the cursor to GEN-ERAL LEDGER.

6. Press [RET] to end the move operation.

When moving a frame in (or into) an outline, the frame is located just after the position of the highlight. The outline should now appear as shown in figure 3.4.

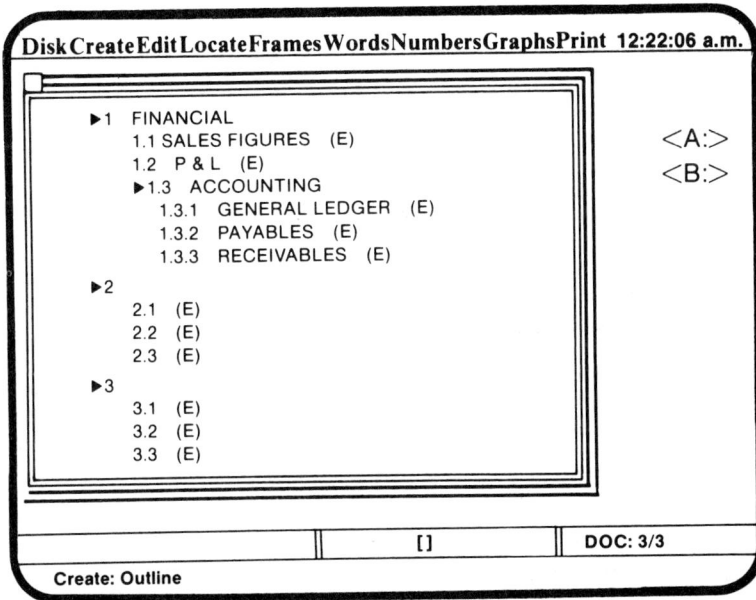

```
┌────────────────────────────────────────────────────────────────┐
│ Disk Create Edit Locate Frames Words Numbers Graphs Print 12:22:06 a.m. │
│ ┌────────────────────────────────────────────────┐             │
│ │ ►1   FINANCIAL                                   │            │
│ │      1.1 SALES FIGURES  (E)                      │   <A:>     │
│ │      1.2  P & L  (E)                             │            │
│ │      ►1.3  ACCOUNTING                            │   <B:>     │
│ │          1.3.1  GENERAL LEDGER  (E)              │            │
│ │          1.3.2  PAYABLES  (E)                    │            │
│ │          1.3.3  RECEIVABLES  (E)                 │            │
│ │ ►2                                               │            │
│ │      2.1  (E)                                    │            │
│ │      2.2  (E)                                    │            │
│ │      2.3  (E)                                    │            │
│ │ ►3                                               │            │
│ │      3.1  (E)                                    │            │
│ │      3.2  (E)                                    │            │
│ │      3.3  (E)                                    │            │
│ └────────────────────────────────────────────────┘             │
│                        []              DOC: 3/3                 │
│ Create: Outline                                                │
└────────────────────────────────────────────────────────────────┘
```

Figure 3.4.   Outline after inserting a section

OUTLINE VIEW AND FRAMES VIEW

In this section we have looked at the outline in only the outline view. However, each section and subsection of the outline is represented by a frame. To see the outline in the frames view, press [F10 View]. Pressing [F10] again returns the screen to the outline view.

All of the operations described above can be performed in the frames view, however the outline view gives a better overall view of the outline. Also, moving around in the outline is easier than moving around in the frames view.

ZOOMING FROM THE OUTLINE TO THE FRAME

You can zoom directly from the outline to a frame with the [F9 Zoom] key. This is convenient, since selecting a frame in the outline and pressing the Zoom key automatically expands the frame to full screen size and moves the cursor into the frame for immediate editing or entering of data or text. Pressing the [F9 Zoom] key again returns you to the outline view.

DISK OPERATIONS

The Disk Pulldown Menu

The Disk pulldown menu is accessed by pressing [INS]. When you press [INS], you are instructing Framework to display one of the pulldown menus. Choose the Disk menu by moving the cursor to the left with the cursor movement keys until the word Disk is highlighted and the Disk menu is displayed. When you have chosen the desired pulldown menu, move the highlight to the desired selection within the menu and press [RET].

A shortcut for making a menu selection is to press [CTRL] and the first letter in the name of the desired menu, in this case D. Options can also be selected within the menu by pressing the first letter of the selection.

The Disk menu operations are described in the following sections.

GET FILE BY NAME

This menu selection allows the operator to retrieve a file directly from disk by typing its name. For example, to retrieve the file "WORD1.FW" from disk to a tray on the desktop, type:

[CTRL] D G WORD1.FW [RET]

Pressing [CTRL] D displays the Disk pulldown menu and G selects "Get File by Name."

SAVE AND CONTINUE

This Disk pulldown menu selection allows the operator to save the file or frame on disk and continue processing. The shortcut method of selecting Save and Continue is:

[CTRL] D S

Pressing [CTRL] D displays the Disk pulldown menu, and S selects "Save and Continue."

It is advisable to frequently save a file that is being processed in memory to disk. Framework has also provided this very simple method:

[CTRL] [RET]

for saving the file in memory to a disk file.

PUT AWAY

The Put Away operation saves (on disk) the frame or frames selected and removes the trays from the desktop.

CLEAN UP DESKTOP

Clean Up Desktop involves moving all of the displayed frames into their trays, but they are not saved on disk.

WRITE DOS TEXT FILE

This disk operation writes selected frames to disk in DOS text format. This command saves files with the filename extension .TXT. *See also* "Printing and Writing to Disk" in the next section on printing.

DOS ACCESS

DOS Access allows access to DOS without leaving Framework. To access DOS you must create an empty word frame and choose DOS Access from the Disk pulldown menu. To create the empty word frame, type:

[CTRL] C E

Pressing [CTRL] C displays the Create pulldown menu, and E selects "Empty / Word Frame." The DOS Access frame can be zoomed to full screen if desired prior to accessing DOS.

To access DOS, type:

[CTRL] D D

Pressing [CTRL] D displays the Disk pulldown menu, and D selects "DOS Access."

The empty word frame is automatically labeled "DOS Access Frame," and all displays appear in this frame until you exit DOS. Programs accessible from DOS may be executed. All visible displays in this frame are saved which allows you to keep a transcript of DOS activities.

To exit DOS and return to Framework, type:

EXIT [RET]

COPYING A FILE FROM ONE DRIVE TO ANOTHER

To copy a file from one drive to another, bring the file from one disk drive to the desktop and then copy the file to the other disk drive from the desktop. For example to copy Word1 from drive B: to drive A:, follow these steps: (Assume that the desktop is empty.)

On the right-hand side of the desktop display, you will see the two disk drive symbols displayed as follows:

```
<A:>
<B:>
```

The cursor will be flashing on one of these disk drive symbols.

1. Display both of the disk directory frames by pressing [RET] and a cursor movement key and [RET] again.

2. Move the cursor to drive B: and press [DOWN-LEVEL] (gray+) to move the cursor into the frame.

3. Select the file Word1 by moving the highlight with the cursor movement keys to that file and pressing [RET]. Word1 will be read into memory trom drive B: and it will be stored in a tray in the lower right-hand corner of the desktop.

4. With the cursor flashing on the tray labeled Word1, press [F8 COPY].

5. Return to the disk frame by pressing [Scroll Lock] and [UPLEVEL] (gray-).

6. Move the cursor to drive A: with the cursor movement key.

7. Move the cursor into the frame of drive A: with the [DOWNLEVEL] (gray +) key.

8. Complete the copy operation by pressing [RET].

DELETING A FILE FROM DISK

To delete a file from a disk, open the disk drive and highlight the file that you wish to delete. Then press the [DEL] key.

Framework will then ask, "Delete from DISK (not undoable) (Y/N)?." Press Y to delete the file.

You may delete more than one (adjacent) file if you use the F6 Extend Select key, prior to pressing [DEL].

PRINTING

Framework prints all types of frames. In this section on printing, the rudiments of printing will be explained that pertain to Framework in general. The details of printing that relate more specifically to spreadsheets, database and graphics will be covered in the chapters on those subjects.

The Print Pulldown Menu

Printing with Framework is accomplished by using the Print pulldown menu. For example, to print the files Word1 and Word2 (these files were created in chapter 2), retrieve these files from disk and store them in trays on the desktop. Now follow these steps:

1. Use the cursor movement keys to highlight the file Word1.
2. Use the [F6 Extend Select] key and the cursor movement keys to also highlight the file Word2.
3. Press [INS] and use the cursor movement keys to select the Print menu.
4. Use the cursor movement keys to select Begin. Press [RET].

A "Preparing to print" message will be displayed at the bottom of the screen. When printing starts you may return to processing.

Explanations of the selections from the Print pulldown menu follow.

BEGIN

This selection starts printing the selected files. If more than one file is selected (with the F6 Extend-Select key), all files will be printed in the order they appear on the desktop. Files are first stored on disk and printing is performed from the disk so that processing can continue. Changes made to a file being printed will not appear until the file is again selected for printing using the Print menu.

If there is not sufficient space to store the files on disk for printing, then the files will be printed from the desktop (memory). In this case, processing must wait until printing is completed. Press [CTRL][Break] to cancel printing from the desktop.

STOP

Stop printing. This selection cancels all current printing requests. Printing may not stop immediately due to the printer's buffer, but printing will stop when your printer is ready to receive more data. If Framework is printing from the desktop (memory), press [CTRL][Break] to cancel printing.

PAUSE

Stop printing until Pause is selected again. Pause is a toggle whose default value is off. If you select Pause while printing is in process, the printer will stop printing and wait. Printing can then be restarted by selecting Pause again.

WAIT FOR EACH PAGE

Stop printing at the end of each page. This control is useful if you wish to change sheets after each page is printed. Since printing occurs from the desktop when this command is used, processing cannot continue until printing is completed. To cancel printing, press [CTRL] [Break]. This toggle must be on before Begin is specified.

DESTINATION OF PRINTOUT

This selection from the Print pulldown menu displays a submenu of output destinations. The choices are First printer, Second printer, Plotter, and DOS text file (*See* "Printing and Writing to Disk" later in this section). To access the Destination of Printout submenu, press either [RET] or [DOWNLEVEL] (gray+). To return to the pulldown menu from the submenu, press the right arrow key (→).

OUTPUT OPTIONS

This selection displays a submenu of output options. Again these can be accessed by pressing [RET] or [DOWN-LEVEL]. The sub-menu is exited by pressing the right arrow key (→). The Output Options menu items are described below:

> **Begin On Page** {1}
> **End After Page** {9999}

These selections allow you to print a specific range of pages within a document. However, once a frame within a containing frame has been selected for printing, that frame and all enclosed frames are printed, regardless of the page range selected.

Keep in mind that Framework allows for the numbering of pages with printing functions. Therefore if you wish to start printing the fourth page of a document whose pages are numbered from 11 to 20, you would specify that printing was to begin on page 14.

Number Of Copies {1}

You can select the number of copies of the document to be printed.

Skip Closed Frames

This is a toggle. When "ON," closed frames are not printed.

Formulas Only

This is also a toggle. If the toggle is "ON," only the print functions and formulas in a frame are printed. If the frame is a spreadsheet, the frame name and cell coordinate print before each formula. The formulas are printed in a column.

Print Frame Labels

This is a toggle which allows you to suppress the printing of frame labels. If a frame label is printed, a blank line precedes and follows the name. Frame labels are always printed in outline view.

Printing Outlines

Framework provides a great deal of flexibility in formatting and printing outlines. You can print outlines with or without section and subsection numbers. You can control the amount of detail by closing containing frames which contain subsections or details that you wish to omit. You can print the outline with page numbers so that it becomes a table of contents. You can suppress frame types and section numbers.

To print an outline of any document with frames within frames, follow these steps:

1. Bring the document to the desktop.
2. If the document is in the "Frames" view, press [F10 View] to change to outline view.
3. Press [INS] and use the cursor movement keys to select the Print menu.
4. Use the cursor movement keys to select BEGIN. Press [RET] and the outline will be printed.

To illustrate outline printing and some of its variations, use the file "Outline1" created earlier in this section. The above four steps should produce a printed copy as shown in figure 3.5.

```
1   FINANCIAL
    1.1   SALES FIGURES   (E)
    1.2   P & L   (E)
    1.3   ACCOUNTING
          1.3.1   GENERAL LEDGER   (E)
          1.3.2   PAYABLES   (E)
          1.3.3   RECEIVABLES   (E)
2
    2.1   (E)
    2.2   (E)
    2.3   (E)
3
    3.1   (E)
    3.2   (E)
    3.3   (E)
```

Figure 3.5.   Printed outline

Now select the Frames menu and move the highlight to the toggle for Number Labels. Press [RET] to turn the toggle "OFF." (The default value is "ON.")

Now select the Frames menu again and move the highlight to the toggle for **Reveal Type**. Press [RET] to turn the toggle "OFF" (The default value is "ON.")

Use the shortcut method [CTRL] P B to print the outline. It should appear as shown in figure 3.6.

```
FINANCIAL
    SALES FIGURES
    P & L
    ACCOUNTING
        GENERAL LEDGER
        PAYABLES
        RECEIVABLES
```

Figure 3.6. Outline with Number Labels and Reveal Type suppressed

To suppress some of the details of the outline, close the containing frame "ACCOUNTING" as follows:

1. Select the **Frames** menu and turn "OFF" the **Number Values** and **Reveal Type** toggles.
2. In the outline view, move the cursor with the [DOWNLEVEL] (gray plus) key and the cursor movement keys until the frame labeled ACCOUNTING is highlighted.

3. Press [RET] to close the containing frame.

4. Move the highlight back to the border of OUTLINE1 and use [CTRL] P to choose the Print menu.

5. Use the cursor movement keys to select the Output Options submenu. Press [RET].

6. Use the cursor movement keys to select the Skip Closed Frames option and press [RET] to change the toggle to "ON." (The default value is "OFF.") Press the right arrow key (→) to close the submenu.

7. Use the cursor movement keys to select BEGIN from the Print menu. Be certain that the highlight is on the border of OUTLINE1 and press [RET]. The printed output should now appear as shown in figure 3.7.

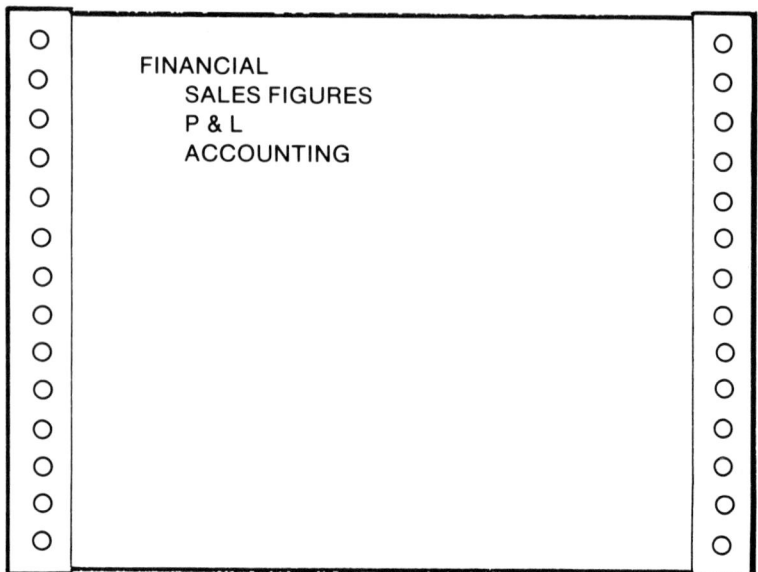

```
FINANCIAL
    SALES FIGURES
    P & L
    ACCOUNTING
```

Figure 3.7. Outline with closed frames skipped

To reopen the closed frames, choose the Frames menu and select Open All.

Printing A Table of Contents

Printing a table of contents is much like printing an outline, but the page numbers are added. To illustrate this, bring Outline1 to the desktop and select the Outline view by pressing [F10-View] (if necessary).

Choose the Frames menu and select the toggle View Page Numbers. Press [RET] to turn the toggle "ON." The default value is "OFF." Notice that page numbers are supplied to all frames including those frames that have not been labeled.

To delete the unused frames, move the highlight to the unwanted frames and press [Del].

To print the outline with page numbers, choose the Print menu and select Begin. The outline should appear as shown in figure 3.8.

```
FINANCIAL  ----------------------  1
    SALES FIGURES  ------------  1
    P & L  --------------------  1
    ACCOUNTING  --------------  1
        GENERAL LEDGER  -------  1
        PAYABLES  -------------  1
        RECEIVABLES  ---------  1
```

Figure 3.8. Table of contents

In this example all sections start on page 1. This is because all frames are empty. If the frames included enough text to fill more than one page, this would be reflected in the table of contents. The table of contents indicates the starting page numbers of the respective frames.

If you edit the document while the page numbers are displayed, they do not update until you again select View Page Numbers from the Frames menu.

Printing Free Floating Frames

Frames may be column arranged or free floating. When printing a containing frame which contains free floating frames, the printed output will be similar to the screen display. That is, the free floating frames will be printed in the same relative position in which they appear on the screen. Also, only the contents of each frame that are visible on the screen will be printed.

If you wish to print the entire contents of a free floating frame (within a containing frame), you must either increase its size or print it as an individual frame. Otherwise, you must change it to a column arranged frame. Note that frames within a free floating frame are always printed as if they are free floating frames.

To change a frame from "column arranged" to "free floating," choose the Frames menu and select the appropriate command. The choices are Put into Column or Allow Free Dragging.

Printing File Directories

File directories can be printed by moving the cursor to the border of the disk drive display and then choosing the Print menu and selecting Begin.

Printing And Writing To Disk

If you wish to examine your printed output without taking the time to have it printed, Framework provides a convenient method. You can print your document to disk using the Print menu's Destination of Output option, DOS Text File. To use this option, follow these steps:

1. Select the document that you wish to print by moving the cursor to the border of the frame.

2. Choose the Print menu by pressing [INS] and moving the highlight to Print.

3. Move the highlight to the bottom of the Print menu and select Destination of Printout by pressing [RET].

4. Move the highlight to DOS Text File and toggle "ON" by pressing [RET] (The default setting is "OFF"). Press the right arrow key (→) to exit this submenu.

5. Select Begin with the cursor movement keys and press [RET] to start printing to disk.

The document will be printed to disk and will be given the same name, but with the extension ".prt" instead of ".fw."

To view the document, load it to the desktop from the disk drive just as you would any other file. When you display the file on the screen, it will show headers, footers, and page offset just as if it were on the printed page.

Printing Functions

Printing functions allow you to control the printed output of the document through the use of formulas. Headers, footers, page numbering, page offset, line spacing, and line length are all controlled by printing functions.

Printing functions are controlled by formulas which are written and stored "behind" the frame label. There are rules of syntax which apply to these formulas.

PRINTING FUNCTION RULES

1. Formulas are entered by moving the highlight to the frame border, pressing [F2-Edit Formula] and then typing the formula. Press [RET] to complete the entry.

2. Printing functions apply to the frame in which they reside and to all subframes when printing in the frames view. In the outline view, the only printing functions that are used are those in the outermost frame selected.

3. Printing functions in a subframe override those functions in the containing frame until the subframe has completed printing.

4. A printing formula begins with the @ sign. The @ sign is followed by the printing command and an open parenthesis, (.

5. Constants, reserved words, and other @ functions are enclosed within the parenthesis. The formula always ends with a closed parenthesis.

6. Constants or the actual text you wish to print are always enclosed with quotation marks.

7. Multiple formulas may be entered in a frame. Formulas must be separated by a comma. You may use [F9-ZOOM] to enlarge the display of the formula.

The various printing functions are described in this chapter's remaining sections.

HEADERS

Headers are used to place constant information, such as chapter names, dates or page numbers, at the top of each page of a document. Printing functions specify the content and position of the constant information that is to be printed.

Consider the following formula for example:

@hc("CHAPTER ONE")

@hc is the header center command. This command causes the header to be positioned in the page's center between the beginning and ending points of the specified print line.

When the preceding example is executed, the header will be printed on line 3, the default print line for headers. The following command will print a centered two line header beginning on line 4:

@hp(4),@hc("CHAPTER ONE
HAVING FUN WITH FRAMEWORK")

In the preceding example, @hp(4) specified that the header will start printing on line 4, and @hc instructs Framework to center the two line header. Observe the following procedure when entering a multiline header:

1. Enter the first header line as usual, but don't press [RET].
2. Press [F9-Zoom]. The formula appears in the expanded frame.
3. Press [RET] to move to a new line. Enter the desired additional lines.
4. Press [F9-Zoom].
5. Press [RET].
6. Print the frame as usual.

Sometimes reserved words may be used in formulas to specify dates or page numbers, as in this example:

@hc("Chapter One "&@date1(@today))

This formula specifies that "Chapter One" and today's date (printed in date1 format) are to be centered in line 3.

The following is another example of a header formula using reserved words:

@pl(30),@hr("Page "&@pn&" of 6",#even)*

In this formula, the page number is to be printed on the right side of line 3 in the format "Page 1 of 6." The #even expression specifies that this header is printed only on even numbered pages. Use the #odd expression to print on odd numbered pages only. If neither is used, printing will occur on both even and odd numbered pages.

The reserved words for formatting the date are as follows:

@date1	Jan 1, 1985
@date2	Jan 1985
@date3	Jan 1
@date4	January 1, 1985

---

* The header and footer commands will not print if @tm(0) or @bm(0) are used. Headers and footers print 3 lines from the top or bottom of the page by default, so these lines must be available.

The header printing functions follow:

header left @hl	Prints the header aligned with the page offset. @hl("Chapter One")
header center @hc	Prints the header centered between the page offset and the right margin (word processing)* or line length (data base and spreadsheet). @hc("Chapter One")
header right @hr	Prints the header aligned with the right margin (word processing) or line length (data base and spreadsheet). @hr("Chapter One")
header position @hp	Prints the header on the specified line. The default value is 3. @hp(4),@hr("Chapter One")
header start @hf	Starts printing the header on the page number specified. @hf(3),@hc("Chapter One")
number pages @pn	Use @pn in headers or footers to have Framework automatically number pages. @hc(@pn)
even/odd #even #odd	Use #even to print the header or footer on even numbered pages only. Use #odd to print header or footer on odd numbered pages only. Default prints on both pages. @hc("Chapter One",#odd)

---

* The right margin or left margin in a word processing document can be set by selecting the desired action from the Words menu (*see* chapter 4).

FOOTERS

Footer formulas are similar to header formulas. The footer printing functions follow:

footer left @fl	Prints the footer aligned with the page offset. @fl("Chapter One")
footer center @fc	Prints the footer centered between the page offset and the right margin (word processing)* or line length (data base and spreadsheet). @fc("Chapter One")
footer right @fr	Prints the footer aligned with the right margin (word processing) or line length (data base and spreadsheet). @fr("Chapter One")
footer position @fp	Prints the footer the specified number of lines from the bottom of the page. The default value is 3. @fp(4),@fr("Chapter One")
footer start @hf	Starts printing the footer on the page number specified. @hf(3),@fc("Chapter One")
number pages @pn	Use @pn in headers or footers to have Framework automatically number pages. @fc(@pn)
even/odd #even #odd	Use #even to print header or footer on even numbered pages only. Use #odd to print header or footer on odd numbered pages only. Default prints on both pages. @fc("Chapter One",#odd)

* The right or left margin in a word processing document can be set by selecting the desired action from the Words menu (*see* chapter 4).

PAGE SETTINGS

new page @np	Start printing this frame at the top of a new page. A number in parentheses following this command instructs Framework to use this number as the new page number. @np(10)*
keep @kp	Keep the contents of the indicated frame all on one page. Causes the current frame to begin in the next page if it cannot be accommodated on the existing page. @kp
skip lines @sk	Skip the specified number of lines before printing the contents of this frame. @sk(10)
line spacing @sp	Specifies line spacing. @sp(2)
top margin @tm	Specify the number of lines in the top margin. The default value is 6. @tm(5)
bottom margin @bm	Specify the number of lines in the bottom margin. The default value is 6. @bm(4)
page offset @po	Specify the number of spaces from the left edge of the paper to the left margin. The default value is 10 spaces. @po(6)
page length @pl	Sets the total number of lines on the page. The default value is 66. @pl(84)

* In our work with @np, we found that the new page sometimes appeared one page later. Also, in some instances @np caused termination of auto page numbering.

line length @ll	Sets the total number of characters that will be printed from the page offset to the end of each line. The default is 65. @ll is generally used to split a wide spreadsheet or a data base table. We found that this command had no effect with word processing frames. @ll(60)

OTHER PRINTING FUNCTIONS

set up printer @st({n})	Sends printer set up codes to the printer. The following example turns on the elite mode on an Epson printer. @st("{ESC}M") Printer functions remain on until they are turned off with another @st function or until the printer is reset manually. Strings must be enclosed within quotation marks in @ st functions. Keystrokes and ASCII codes must be enclosed in brackets { }.
print frame @print(frame name)	Prints the frame specified. @print(CHAP1)

4
Word Processing With Framework

Framework provides a powerful word processor which can be used to create, edit, reformat, save and retrieve documents. This chapter is designed to teach you how to use Framework's word processor software. We assume that you have already mastered the techniques of working with Framework. If you have not, return to chapter 2.

Creating a Document

Let's begin our discussion of Framework's word processor by actually creating a document. First create an empty word frame as follows:

1. Boot the system (if necessary) and load Framework to display the desktop. (*See* chapter 2, Starting a Framework Work Session).

2. Press [INS] to display the Create Menu.

3. Select Empty / Word Frame and press [RET]. An empty word frame should be displayed on the desktop.

4. Label the frame by typing TRY1 [RET] on the frame border.

5. Move the cursor into the frame by pressing [DOWN-LEVEL].

ENTERING TEXT, CURSOR MOVEMENT AND EDITING

Now type the following paragraph:*

This is a document created with the Framework word processor. Notice as you type that the words are not justified, (evenly aligned on the right-hand side of the paragraph). Notice also that it is not necessary to use the Return key at the end of each line. If you just keep typing, the cursor automatically advances to the next line when it reaches the end of the current line.

If your screen display is not an exact duplicate of the example, don't be alarmed. You may have made some spelling errors, or the paragraph format may differ because your margins are different. Also, the right side of your screen is probably not aligned evenly (justified).

---

* Indent the paragraph by pressing the [TAB] key. The [TAB] key is located just above the [Ctrl] key.

To correct mistakes, you can move the cursor to the
incorrect letter and type over it. (Press [F1 Help] to view a help
screen on cursor movement. Select the Index of Topics at the
bottom of the HELP screen to find help on other topics.)
During error correction, notice that new text is inserted and
previously typed text is moved to the right to accommodate the
corrections. Use the [DEL]* key to erase unwanted letters. Use
[CTRL][DEL] to delete an entire word.

The backspace key can also be used to correct typing
errors. The backspace key is the gray ← key located just to the
left of the [Num Lock] key.

So far our corrections have been made in the insert mode.
In this mode, keyboard entries are inserted in the text and
extraneous characters must be deleted. The typeover mode is
also available in Framework's word processing mode. In the
typeover mode, a keyboard entry replaces the character on
which the cursor is positioned.

To change from the insert mode to the typeover mode,
select the **Edit** menu. Select **Typeover** with the highlight and
press [RET]. This sets the typeover mode to "on" (the default is
"off"). Repeating this procedure will return the typeover mode
to "off." A shortcut for setting the typeover toggle is
[CTRL]-E T. *See* "Saving a File, Menu Selection Shortcuts" in
chapter 2.

Now, to reformat the paragraph to appear as it does in the
example we must reset the margins. Follow these steps:

---

* [DEL] and Delete key both refer to the key to the immediate right of [INS].

1. Choose the Words menu by pressing [INS] and moving the highlight to Words on the menu bar.

2. Select Left Margin with the highlight and press [RET]. The cursor will be flashing in the lower left corner of the screen on the number "0."

3. Type the new left margin "6" to change the left margin to 6 spaces from the left side of the document, and press [RET]. The actual position of the left and right margins on the printed page are determined by the page offset. That is, if the page offset is 10 and the left margin is set at 6, then the printed text will be aligned on column 16. *See* "Printing Functions, Page Settings, Page Offset" in chapter 3.

These three steps reformat only the current paragraph when you choose the Words menu. You can reformat the total contents of a frame by positioning the cursor on the frame border before choosing the Words menu.

If you reset the margins while you are entering text, the margin settings are retained until they are reset. That is, all subsequent text entered will conform to the new margin settings.

Repeat the preceding three steps to reset the right margin to 60, but of course this time you must select Right Margin from the Words menu and replace the default value of 65 with the new value of 60.

To "justify" the paragraph, select the Words menu and choose the Justify toggle. When you turn the Justify toggle "on," the Align Left toggle is automatically turned "off," and the current paragraph is justified (aligned evenly on the right).

The document should now appear just as in the example. If you wish to save this frame on disk, press [CTRL] [RET]. *See also* chapter 2 "Saving Frames on Disk."

In this section elements of both the Edit menu and the Words menu were used. A more complete description of these two menus follows. If you feel it is not necessary to study these menus further, then skip to the section entitled "Printing a Document."

The Words Menu

The Words menu can be accessed by pressing [INS] and moving the highlight to Words on the menu bar or by pressing [Ctrl]-W.

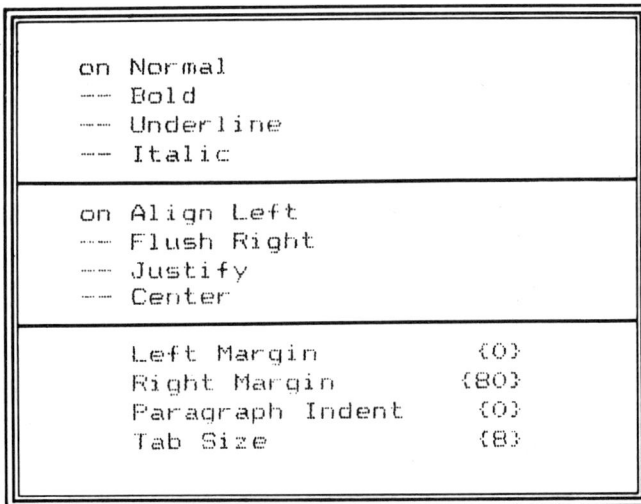

```
on  Normal
---  Bold
---  Underline
---  Italic

on  Align Left
---  Flush Right
---  Justify
---  Center

     Left Margin          {0}
     Right Margin         {80}
     Paragraph Indent     {0}
     Tab Size             {8}
```

Figure 4.1. Words menu

The Words menu is displayed in figure 4.1. It is used to change type styles and reformat paragraphs. What follows is a description of each selection available in the Words menu.

The first four selections from the Words menu are used to control type styles. To change the style of text, first select the text to be changed with [F6 Extend Select], then choose the styling command from the Words menu. To select all text within a frame, select the frame border first. When no text is highlighted, all subsequent text will be styled according to the style selected.

—— NORMAL

This selection is used to reset Bold, Underline, or Italics. The two dashes preceeding the selection indicate that this is a toggle. The first four Words menu selections (Normal, Bold, Underline, and Italic) are toggles. If Normal is turned "on," the Bold, Underline, and Italic will automatically be turned "off."

—— BOLD

If Bold is turned "on" all subsequent text will be bold, but if Bold is specified in the Extend-Select mode, only the high-lighted text will be bold. The boldface text will be displayed on the screen with higher intensity than normal text. Use Normal to reset the Bold toggle to "off."

When using menu selections, remember that the [INS] key always displays the last menu selected. Also, when a menu is displayed, pressing [INS] has the same effect as pressing [RET]. Therefore, if you are using the same command repeatedly, such as Bold, you may highlight the selected text and then simply press [INS] twice to change the selected text to Bold.

—— UNDERLINE

Underline follows the same rules as Bold. When Underline is set "on," all subsequent text (and spaces between words) is underlined. If Underline is used in the Extend-Select mode, only the highlighted text is underlined.

—— ITALIC

Italic follows the same rules as Bold. When Italic is set "on", all subsequent text is displayed on the screen in italic type. If Italic is used in the Extend-Select mode, only the highlighted text is italicized. While the screen displays the selected text in Italic, your printer may display the selected text as underlined.

The following four selections from the Words menu are used to reform paragraphs. Only one of these four toggles may be "on" at a time. If any one is set to "on", the other three will automatically be set to "off." If one of these commands is selected from the frame border, the entire contents of the frame will be affected.

—— ALIGN LEFT

This selection is the normal default setting for text alignment. Left aligned text will left justify lines of text on the left margin.

—— FLUSH RIGHT

This selection will cause text to be aligned on the right margin. This might be useful for aligning the date on the heading of a letter.

—— JUSTIFY

This selection causes both paragraph margins to be aligned, just as in this paragraph. Framework does this by inserting spaces at appropriate positions to "stretch" the lines for alignment.

—— CENTER

This selection centers the text in each line between the page offset and the right margin. This is useful for titles or major headings.

This is an example of a centered line.

The next three selections from the Words menu are used to control the current paragraph (The Tab Size command controls the entire frame). Selections from the frame border will control the contents of the entire frame. More than one paragraph within a frame can be controlled with the use of [F6 Extend Select].

LEFT MARGIN

To change the left margin, press L to select Left Margin. Type in the replacement value followed by [RET]. The actual position of the left and right margins on the printed page are determined by the page offset. If the page offset is 10 and the left margin is set at 6, then the printed text will begin at column 16. *See* "Printing Functions, Page Settings, Page Offset" in chapter 3.

RIGHT MARGIN

To change the right margin, press R to select Right Margin. Type in the replacement value followed by [RET]. The actual position of the left and right margins on the printed page are determined by the page offset. *See* "Printing Functions, Page Settings, Page Offset" in chapter 3.

PARAGRAPH INDENT

Paragraph indent changes the number of spaces that the first line of a paragraph is indented. Change the value by pressing P to select Paragraph Indent from the Words menu and then typing the replacement value followed by [RET]. A negative value will cause the first line to start to the left of the left margin.

TAB SIZE

This selection sets the number of spaces the cursor moves to the right each time the [TAB] key is pressed. The default value is 8. When the Tab Size is changed, it changes for the entire frame, including the text already entered.

The Edit Menu

The Edit menu can be accessed by pressing [INS] and moving the highlight to Edit on the menu bar or by pressing [Ctrl]-E.

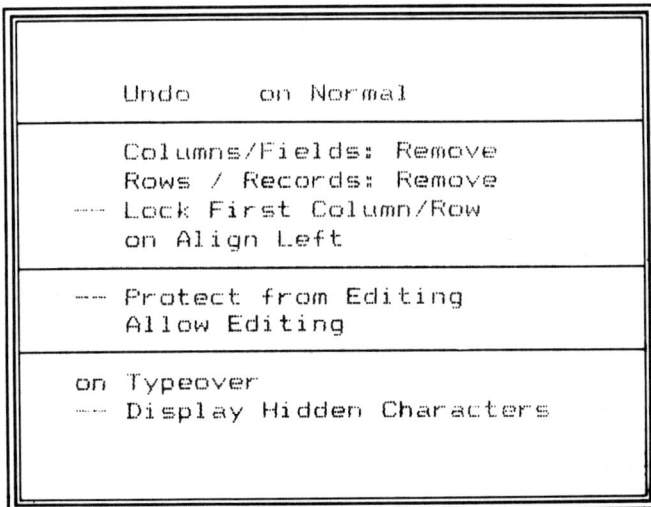

```
    Undo      on Normal

    Columns/Fields: Remove
    Rows / Records: Remove
--- Lock First Column/Row
    on Align Left

--- Protect from Editing
    Allow Editing

on  Typeover
--- Display Hidden Characters
```

Figure 4.2. Edit menu

The Edit menu is displayed in figure 4.2. The items in the Edit menu that pertain to word processing are described below. Those items which pertain to the spreadsheet or data base are explained later in those chapters.

UNDO

This selection allows you to reverse an operation that has already been completed. For instance, if you delete a frame, you may undo the deletion by selecting Undo from the Edit menu. Undo will reverse the last Delete, Move, Sort or Replace command, but it will not reverse a deletion from disk.

—— PROTECT FROM EDITING

This command protects selected frames from editing. This is useful for preventing accidental changes to text.

ALLOW EDITING

This command reverses Protect From Editing.

—— TYPEOVER

This toggle allows text to be replaced as you type. When the toggle is "on," existing text is replaced by new keyboard entries. When the toggle is "off," new characters are inserted within the old text. The default value is "off." The quick method of changing this toggle is to type [CTRL]-E T.

—— DISPLAY HIDDEN CHARACTERS

This selection allows screen display of the hidden characters that Framework uses to edit text. This is sometimes helpful when you experience difficulty editing the text to your own satisfaction. Spaces, tabs, and returns are indicated by special symbols. Page breaks are not revealed.

Advanced Editing

In this section we will practice using the advanced editing features available with Framework's word processor.

We will be working with the document TRY1 created earlier in this chapter (*See* "Entering Text, Cursor Movement and Editing"). If you saved TRY1, bring it back to the desktop as follows:

1. Press [Scroll Lock] to move the cursor to the disk drive selection.

2. With the cursor on drive B: (or the drive containing the file TRY1), press [RET] to display the contents of the selected drive.

3. Press [DOWNLEVEL] to move the cursor into the drive frame.

4. Move the cursor so that the file TRY1.FW is highlighted and press [RET] to bring the file into its tray. Press [RET] again to display the file on the desktop.

5. Press [F9 Zoom] to expand the frame to the full screen. The display should now appear as shown in figure 4.3.

If you did not save TRY1, refer to "Entering Text, Cursor Movement, and Editing" earlier in this chapter. Retype and reform the paragraph so that it appears as shown.

For practice let's change the margins back to the default settings of 0 for the left margin and 65 for the right margin. Follow these steps.

1. With the frame zoomed to full screen and the cursor located in the frame, choose the Words menu, [CTRL] W, and highlight the Left Margin command. Press [RET].

2. Replace the value of 6 with 0, and press [RET] again.

3. Press [INS] to choose the Words menu again, and use the cursor movement keys to select Right Margin. Press [RET].

4. Replace 60 with 65 and press [RET] again. The paragraph should now appear as shown in figure 4.4.

This is a document created with the Framework word
processor. Notice as you type that the words are not
justified,(evenly aligned on the right-hand side of
the paragraph). Notice also that it is not necessary
to use the Return key at the end of each line. If you
just keep typing, the cursor automatically advances to
the next line when it reaches the end of the current
line.

Figure 4.3.   File TRY1

This is a document created with the Framework word
processor. Notice as you type that the words are not
justified,(evenly aligned on the right-hand side of the
paragraph). Notice also that it is not necessary to use the
Return key at the end of each line. If you just keep typing, the
cursor automatically advances to the next line when it reaches
the end of the current line.

Figure 4.4.   Paragraph with left margin reset to 0 and 65

Now let's set the indent and change the paragraph to Align Left. There are two ways to control the indentation of the first line of a paragraph. One way is to set Paragraph Indent from the Words menu to the desired value. The second way is to use the [Tab] key to indent the first line when needed.

The Paragraph Indent setting automatically indents the first line of each paragraph as text is being entered. If you subsequently wish to start a line on the left margin, then Paragraph Indent has to be reset. Paragraph Indent only affects the current paragraph or subsequent paragraphs after the setting has been changed.

The default value for Tab Size is 8; the minimum value is 1. Tab Size affects all tab settings in the current frame. Therefore, if you have been using the tab key to indent, changing the Tab Size setting in the Words menu will change the indentation of all paragraphs in the frame, including those previously entered.

Follow these steps to set indentation and to set justify "off:"

1. With the cursor located in the paragraph TRY1, choose the Words menu, and highlight Paragraph Indent.

2. Press [RET] and replace the value 0 with the value 5. Press [RET] again. Notice that the indentation did not change. This is because the original paragraph was indented with the [Tab] key.

3. Move the cursor to the first line of the paragraph and press [Home]. Notice the cursor moves to position 5. Now press [DEL] and the first line reforms to the indented position. The paragraph should now appear as shown in figure 4.5.

```
     This is a document created with the Framework word
processor.   Notice as you type that the  words  are  not
justified,(evenly  aligned   on  the  right-hand  side  of  the
paragraph).  Notice  also  that it is  not necessary to  use the
Return key at the end of each line.  If you just keep typing, the
cursor  automatically advances to the next  line  when it reaches
the end of the current line.
```

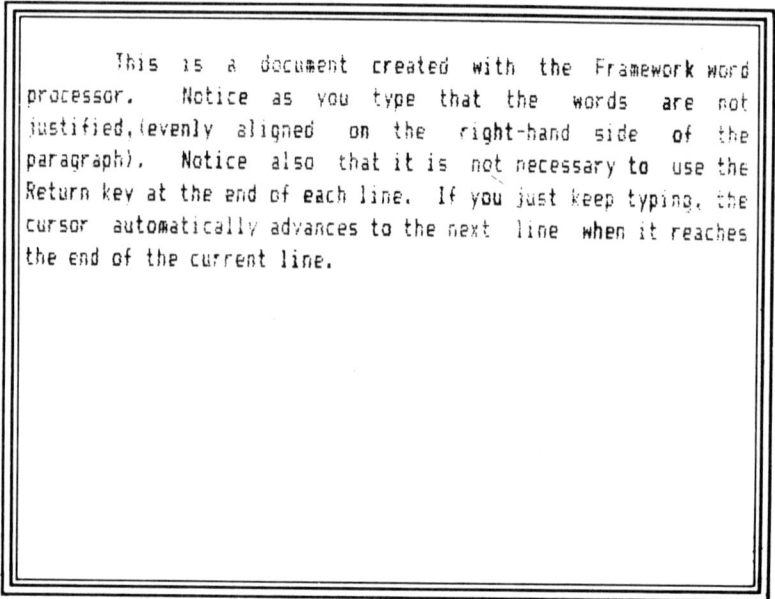

Figure 4.5. Paragraph TRY1 with Paragraph Indent 5

MOVING, COPYING AND DELETING TEXT

The procedures for moving and copying text are similar. First select the text to be moved or copied by highlighting the words or lines with [F6 Extend Select]. Then move the cursor to the new position in the text. [RET] completes the move.

To demonstrate this technique, bring the file TRY1 to the desktop and move the cursor into the frame. Now follow these steps:

1. Move the cursor to the beginning of the paragraph and press [F6-Extend Select].

2. Now use the following keystrokes to highlight the first two sentences.

[↓]		Moves cursor down and highlights first line.
[↓]		Moves cursor down and highlights second line.
[↓]		Moves cursor down and highlights third line.
[Ctrl]	[←]	Press this key combination 10 times to remove the highlight from "Notice also that it is not necessary to use the"

3. Press [F7-Move] to choose the move command.

4. Move the cursor to the end of the text.

5. Press [RET] to complete the move operation. The first two sentences are moved to the end of the paragraph. The paragraph should now appear as shown in figure 4.6.

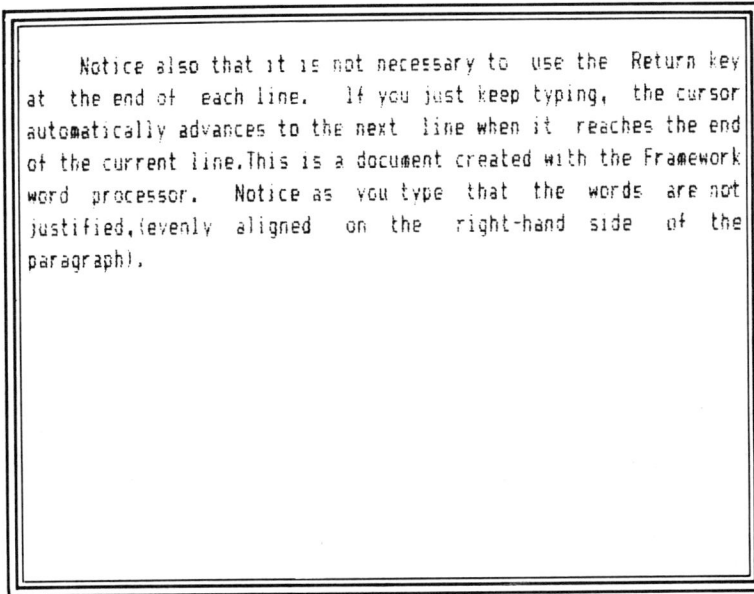

```
    Notice also that it is not necessary to  use the  Return key
at  the end of  each line.   If you just keep typing,  the cursor
automatically advances to the next  line when it  reaches the end
of the current line.This is a document created with the Framework
word  processor.   Notice as  you type  that  the  words  are not
justified,(evenly  aligned   on   the   right-hand  side   of  the
paragraph).
```

Figure 4.6. Paragraph TRY1 with first two sentences moved

Now use the same procedure to copy the remainder of the paragraph to the position immediately following the two sentences just moved. Use these steps:

1. Move the cursor to the beginning of the paragraph.
2. Press [F6-Extend Select].
3. Use the cursor movement keys to highlight the text to the end of the second sentence.
4. Press [F8-Copy].
5. Move the cursor to the end of the text "paragraph.)" and press [RET] to complete the copy.

The paragraph should now appear as in figure 4.7.

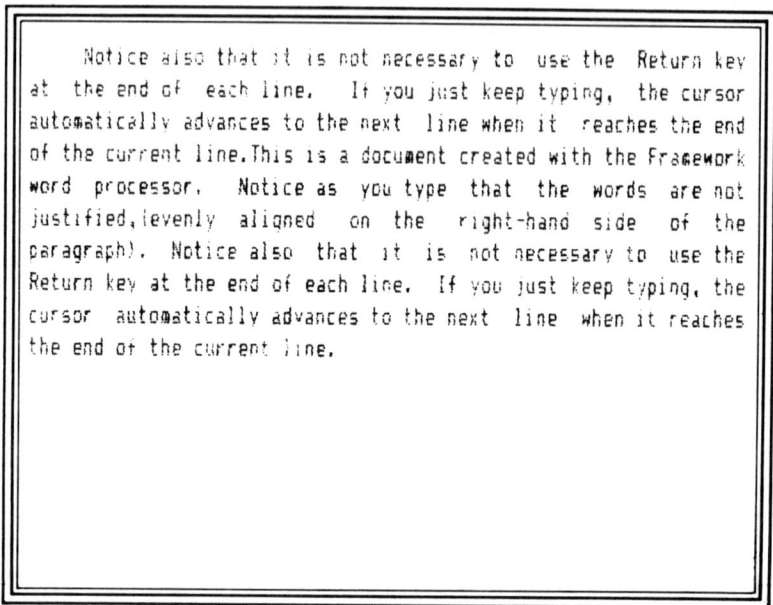

```
      Notice also that it is not necessary to  use the  Return key
at  the end of  each line.   If you just keep typing,  the cursor
automatically advances to the next  line when it  reaches the end
of the current line.This is a document created with the Framework
word  processor.   Notice as  you type  that  the  words  are not
justified,ievenly  aligned    on  the   right-hand  side    of  the
paragraph).  Notice also  that  it  is  not necessary to  use the
Return key at the end of each line.  If you just keep typing, the
cursor  automatically advances to the next  line  when it reaches
the end of the current line.
```

Figure 4.7.   Paragraph TRY1 after copy

To delete the first four lines of the paragraph, highlight the text you wish to delete and press [DEL]. The paragraph should now appear as shown in figure 4.5. Remember that [DEL] will delete all of the highlighted text. Also, use [CTRL][DEL] to delete one word at a time.

SEARCH AND REPLACE

The Search and Replace commands are situated on the Locate menu (*see* figure 4.8).

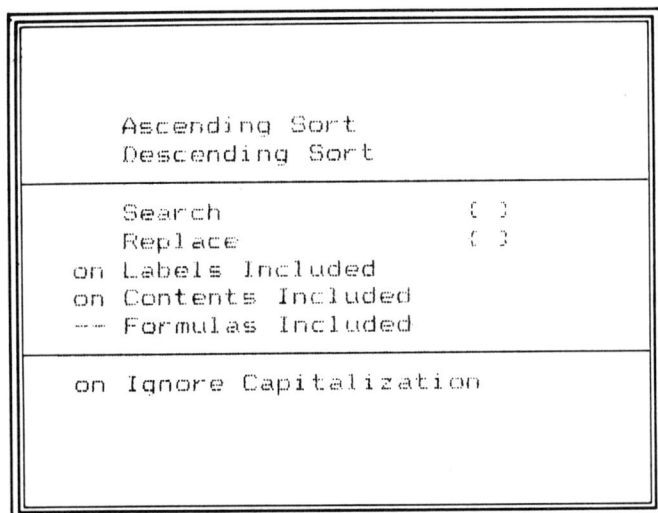

```
          Ascending Sort
          Descending Sort

          Search                    ( )
          Replace                   ( )
     on   Labels Included
     on   Contents Included
     --   Formulas Included

     on   Ignore Capitalization
```

Figure 4.8.   Locate menu

These commands are used to search parts of or entire documents, including frame labels if desired, to find a word or · phrase. Framework includes "wild cards" to help you find words that may be spelled similarly. To illustrate the use of Search and Replace, load the file TRY1 (figure 4.5) to the desktop and follow these steps:

1. With the cursor inside the TRY1 frame, choose the Locate menu and highlight the Replace command.

2. Press [RET] to choose Replace. The cursor will move to the lower left corner of the screen.

The first two steps can be abbreviated by pressing [CTRL]-[L] [R].

3. Enter the text to be searched for. In this case type evenly. Press [RET].

4. Framework now asks for the replacement text. Type unevenly and press [RET]. The highlight will imme- diately move to the first occurrence of the search word and stop. Choose one of the options indicated in the message area at the bottom of the screen.

[RET]	Replace and Find Next
[↓]	Find Next (cursor down)
[Home]	Replace and Stay
[End]	Replace all
[ESC]	To exit

5. Press [RET] to replace "evenly" with "unevenly" and continue the search. Since there is only one occur- rence of the search word, Framework will display the final message "Not found again."

If you choose the Search command instead of the Replace command in the above steps, Framework will only prompt for the "search" word. When the highlight moves to the first occur- rence of the search word, the following choices are available:

[↑]	Find Previous (cursor up)
[↓]	Find Next (cursor down)
	Any other key to exit.

The search will include frame labels, frame contents, and frame formulas if these toggles are on. The default values are shown for these three toggles in figure 4.8.

SEARCH WILD CARDS

The symbols "*" and "?" are the search wild cards. Use "*" to search for any group of letters and use "?" to search for any one letter. For example, the search word "t?o" would find the words *"too"* and *"two,"* The search word "t*o" would find the word *"to,"* a portion of the word *"through,"* and a segment of a phrase such as *"time o*ut."

Printing A Document and Other Options

In chapter 3, printing was described as it applies to Framework in general. In this chapter, an example of controlling printed output will be presented.

First we will build a document using multiple frames. Then headings and footings will be illustrated, followed by page numbering and page settings. Finally, an illustration of printed output to disk will be presented.

WORKING WITH MULTIPLE FRAMES

Multiple frames can be very useful when processing data with Framework. For instance suppose you wanted to include a spreadsheet frame in your word processing document. Frame types cannot be moved. In other words only Word frames can be used in the word processing environment. If you wish to include a data base frame or a spreadsheet frame in your document, you must create another frame for these.

Multiple frames can also be useful when printed output is being edited. Since editing is accomplished by using print commands on the frame formula, it is necessary to create a new frame for this purpose.

The following examples will demonstrate the use of multiple frames:

1. Create an empty word frame, and label it PRINT1. Then use [DOWNLEVEL] to move the cursor into the frame's body. Now create and label three word subframes within PRINT1. Label them FRAME1, FRAME2, and FRAME3.

2. Press the Up arrow key twice followed by [DOWN-LEVEL] to move the cursor into FRAME1. Type the following text and follow the instructions given:

   This is an example of the use
   of multiple frames. Change
   the right margin to 30 with
   the Words menu. Note that
   this frame contains 6 lines of
   text.

3. Press [UPLEVEL] to move to FRAME1's border. Press the Down arrow key followed by [DOWN-LEVEL] to move the cursor into FRAME2. Type the following text:

   This is the second frame. Use the Words
   menu again to change the right margin to
   40. Notice the spacing between frames
   on the printed output. This frame
   contains 5 lines of text.

4. Press [UPLEVEL], Down arrow, and [DOWNLEVEL] to move the cursor into FRAME3. Type the following text:

   This is the third frame.
   Select "justified" from the
   Words menu to make the lines
   align evenly on the right
   margin. Change the right
   margin to 30. This frame
   contains 7 lines of text.

5. Press [UPLEVEL], Up arrow, Up arrow, [UPLEVEL] to move the cursor to the border of PRINT1. Then press [F10-VIEW]. The display should appear as shown in figure 4.9.

6. Press [F10-VIEW] again. Then select the Print menu and print the document. The printed output should appear as shown in figure 4.10. You must be in the frames view to print the contents of a frame.

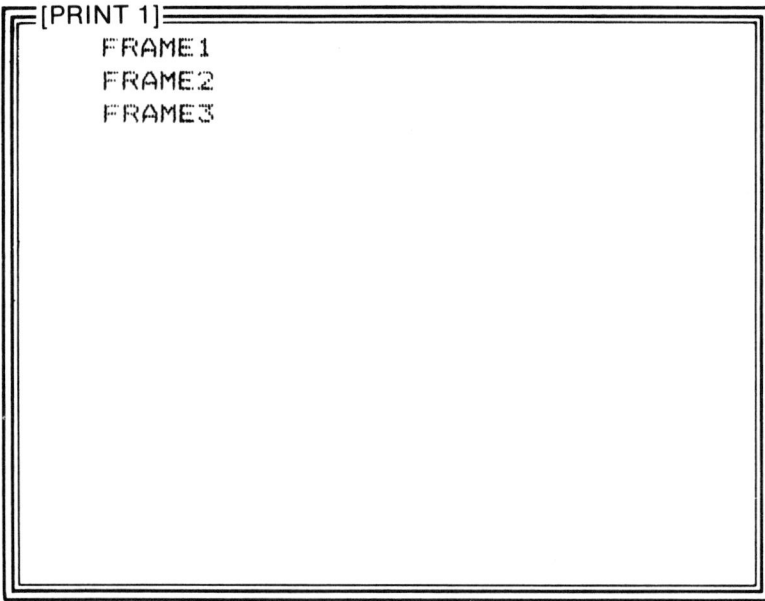

```
[PRINT 1]
    FRAME 1
    FRAME 2
    FRAME 3
```

Figure 4.9. Frame PRINT1 in outline view

The printed output in figure 4.10 displayed the frame labels. In most cases, these are not needed. To hide the frame labels, choose the "Output Options" submenu from the Print menu. Choose "Print Frame Labels" from this submenu to turn the toggle "off". The printed output should now appear as shown in figure 4.11.

```
FRAME1

This is an example of the use
of multiple frames.  Change
the right margin to 30 with
the Words Menu.  Note that
this frame contains 6 lines of
text.

FRAME2

This is the second frame.  Use the Words
Menu again to change the right margin to
40.  Notice the spacing between frames
on the printed output.  This frame
contains 5 lines of text.

FRAME3

This   is   the   third   frame.
Select   "justified"   from   the
Words Menu   to   make the lines
align   evenly   on   the   right
margin.     Change   the   right
margin   to   30.     This   frame
contains 7 lines of text.
```

Figure 4.10.   Printed output of PRINT1

```
This is an example of the use
of multiple frames.  Change
the right margin to 30 with
the Words Menu.  Note that
this frame contains 6 lines of
text.

This is the second frame.  Use the Words
Menu again to change the right margin to
40.  Notice the spacing between frames
on the printed output.  This frame
contains 5 lines of text.

This   is   the   third   frame.
Select   "justified"   from   the
Words Menu   to   make the lines
align   evenly   on   the   right
margin.     Change   the   right
margin   to   30.     This   frame
contains 7 lines of text.
```

Figure 4.11.   Printed output of PRINT1 with Print Frame
Labels "off"

Notice that two lines appear between frames. Although two lines is normal spacing between frames, this spacing can be overridden if desired.

Sometimes you will want to invoke print commands in the middle of a paragraph. Since print commands can only be placed in frame formulas in the frame border, it is necessary to start a new frame and eliminate the spacing between frames.

To eliminate the spacing between the frames in Print1, follow these steps:

1. Display PRINT1 in the frames view, then press [F9-ZOOM]. FRAME1 and FRAME2 should be displayed on the screen.

2. Choose the Frames menu and turn on the toggle, Allow Free Dragging.

3. Press the Down arrow key to move the cursor to the border of FRAME2 and press [F3-DRAG].

4. Now drag FRAME2 vertically using the [↑] (cursor up) key until the ghost border is overlaying the last line of text in FRAME1. Press [RET].

5. Repeat steps 3 and 4 above to drag FRAME3 up to the last line of text of FRAME2.

6. Now move the cursor to the border of PRINT1 and choose the Print menu to print the document. The printed output should now appear as shown in figure 4.12.

Finally, figure 4.13 illustrates that creative arrangements of frames can be produced using [F3-DRAG].

```
This is an example of the use
of multiple frames.  Change
the right margin to 30 with
the Words Menu.  Note that
this frame contains 6 lines of
text.
This is the second frame.  Use the Words
Menu again to change the right margin to
40.   Notice the spacing between frames
on the printed output.  This frame
contains 5 lines of text.
This is the third frame.
Select "justified"  from the
Words Menu to make the lines
align evenly on the right
margin.  Change the right
margin to 30.  This frame
contains 7 lines of text.
```

Figure 4.12.   Printed output of PRINT1 with frames dragged

```
This is an example of the use
of multiple frames.  Change
the right margin to 30 with        This  is    the    third  frame.
the Words Menu.  Note that         Select   "justified"  from  the
this frame contains 6 lines of     Words  Menu to make  the lines
text.                              align   evenly   on   the  right
                                   margin.   Change   the   right
                                   margin   to   30.    This  frame
                                   contains 7 lines of text.

This is the second frame.  Use the Words
Menu again to change the right margin to
40.   Notice the spacing between frames
on the printed output.  This frame
contains 5 lines of text.
```

Figure 4.13.   Dragging frames for creative arrangements

HEADINGS AND FOOTINGS

Headings and footings are useful for giving a multipage document continuity. They can also be used to print a slogan on each page of the document. Page numbering and dating can also be accomplished using heading and footing commands.

Heading and footing commands are entered into the frame formula with the [F2-Formula Edit] key.

To illustrate the use of headings and footings commands, create an empty word frame, label it PRINT2, and type the following:

```
This is an illustration of heading and footing commands. Use the
Words menu to set the left margin to 12 and the right margin to
52. Keep in mind that the default value for the top margin is 6
lines, and the default value for the bottom margin is 4 lines.
The default value for the header print line is 3 lines (from the
top) and the default value for the footer print position is 3
lines (from the bottom).
```

To enter a three line header starting on line 2 of the document, follow these steps:

1. Move the cursor to the border of the frame PRINT2.
2. Press [F2-Edit Formula] and [F9-ZOOM]; then enter the following:

@hp(2),@hc("HAVING FUN WITH FRAMEWORK [RET]

HEADERS AT THE TOP [RET]

FOOTERS AT THE BOTTOM") [F5-Recalc]

In the above commands, @hp(2) is the command which tells Framework to position the header in line 2. The command @hc tells Framework to center the header described in the parenthesis. Pressing [RET] causes the header to be continued on the next line, and [F5-Recalc] ends the formula. If you were entering a one line header, it would not be necessary to use [F9-Zoom] and the header would be ended with [RET].

Now use the Print menu to print the document PRINT2. It should appear as shown in figure 4.14.

```
          HAVING FUN WITH FRAMEWORK
             HEADERS AT THE TOP
            FOOTERS AT THE BOTTOM


     This is an illustration of heading and
     footing commands.  Use the Words Menu to
     set the left margin to 12 and the right
     margin to 52.  Keep in mind that the
     default value for the top margin is 6
     lines, and the default value for the
     bottom margin is 4 lines.  The default
     value for the header print line is 3
     lines (from the top) and the default
     value for the footer print position is 3
     lines (from the bottom).
```

Figure 4.14. PRINT2 showing three line header

To create a footer containing a constant text, today's date and the page number, follow these steps:

1. Move the cursor to the border of the frame PRINT2.
2. Press [F2-Formula Edit] and [F9-Zoom].
3. Move the cursor to the end of the print commands, enter a comma after the last entry, and type the following:

@pl(23),@fc("FOOTER EXAMPLE [RET]
PAGE NO. "&@PN&"OF 10 &@DATE1(@TODAY)) [RET]

In the above commands, @pl(23) changes the page length to 23 lines. The command @fc centers the footer described in the parenthesis. Pressing [RET] starts another line of the footer.

The command @pn creates automatic page numbering. @DATE1 formats the date and @TODAY causes the system date to be printed in the prescribed format.

The total formula should appear as follows:

@hp(2),@hc("HAVING FUN WITH FRAMEWORK
HEADERS AT THE TOP
FOOTERS AT THE BOTTOM"),
@pl(23),@fc("FOOTER EXAMPLE
PAGE NO. "&@PN&"OF 10" &@DATE1(@TODAY))

The printed document should now appear as shown in figure 4.15.

```
        HAVING FUN WITH FRAMEWORK
          HEADERS AT THE TOP
         FOOTERS AT THE BOTTOM


This is an illustration of heading and
footing commands.  Use the Words Menu to
set the left margin to 12 and the right
margin to 52.  Keep in mind that the
default value for the top margin is 6
lines, and the default value for the
bottom margin is 4 lines.  The default
value for the header print line is 3
lines (from the top) and the default
value for the footer print position is 3
lines (from the bottom).



            FOOTER EXAMPLE
 PAGE NO.  1 of 10  Jan 28, 1985
```

Figure 4.15.   Printed output showing footer with page
                   numbering and date

PRINTED OUTPUT TO DISK

It is possible with Framework to view printed output
without actually printing. By using the "Destination of Printout" from the Print menu, an image of the document is created
in a DOS text file so that you can preview the printed output
before producing a hard copy.

To create a DOS text file of PRINT2 for viewing, follow
these steps:

1. With the cursor positioned on the border of PRINT2,
   select the Print menu and choose the Destination of
   Output submenu. Be sure you are in the frames view.

2. Select DOS Text File from the submenu by pressing
   [RET] to turn on the toggle.

3. Return the cursor to Begin at the top of the Print
   menu and press [RET].

The file PRINT2.FW will be "printed" to disk, and the
disk file will be labeled PRINT2.PRT.
To view the file, load the file PRINT2.PRT from the disk
just as you would any other file.

5

The Framework Spreadsheet

Introduction

The Framework spreadsheet is a powerful electronic spreadsheet. Users familiar with Lotus® and VisiCalc® will find the spreadsheet frame very similar. Also, Framework has many advanced features not available on other spreadsheet software.

In this chapter, you will learn how to use the Framework spreadsheet. It is assumed that you have already mastered the techniques of working with Framework. If you have not used Framework before it is suggested that you return to chapter 2.

Creating a Spreadsheet

Create an empty spreadsheet frame as follows:

1. Boot the system (if necessary) and load Framework to display the Framework desktop (See chapter 1, Starting a Framework Worksession).
2. Press [INS] to display the Create Menu.
3. Select Spreadsheet and press [RET]. An empty Spreadsheet will be displayed on the desktop.
4. Label the frame by typing SPREAD1 [RET] on the frame border.
5. Move the cursor into the frame by pressing [Down-level].

Cursor Movement

The function of the cursor movement keys in the spreadsheet is analogous to their function in the word processor. There are a couple of notable exceptions.

When entering data in a column, press [RET] twice: once to store the data in the field and again to move the cursor down one row.

When entering data in a row, press [TAB] to store the data and move the cursor to the right one column. Use [Shift][Tab] to store data and move the cursor one column to the left.

Using this method of cursor movement, the cursor movement keys are free to be used for numeric entries from the numeric keypad. You may toggle the numeric keypad to "numbers only" by pressing [Num Lock].

Refer to table 5.1 for the complete list of cursor movement keys in a spreadsheet.

Table 5.1. Cursor movement in a spreadsheet

[→]	Right one column
[←]	Left one column
[↑]	Up one row
[↓]	Down one row
[RET]	Down one row
[TAB]	Right one column
[Shift]-[TAB]	Left one column
[Home]	Leftmost cell in the current row
[CTRL][HOME]	Top left cell of the spreadsheet
[END]	Rightmost cell in the current row
[CTRL][END]	Bottom right cell in the spreadsheet
[PG UP]	Up one frame
[PG DN]	Down one frame

Entering Text

We will illustrate spreadsheet usage by creating the spreadsheet shown in figure 5.1. To enter titles in the spreadsheet,
SPREAD1, move the cursor to cell B1 and type the following:

JAN [TAB]

The [TAB] key stores the entry and moves the cursor right
one cell.

Now enter the remaining headings as follows:

FEB [TAB]
MAR [TAB]
[SPACEBAR] 1ST QTR [RET] .
[RET] [RET] [HOME]

The spacebar must be pressed before entering "1st QTR". Framework assumes that all entries beginning with a numeric character should be treated as numeric data. Pressing the spacebar instructs Framework to treat the entry as text data. Remember that [RET] completes the entry in a cell, and pressing [RET] twice moves the cursor down two rows. The [HOME] key moves the cursor to the leftmost cell of the current row. The cursor should now be positioned in cell A3.

Now enter the titles for the rows as follows:

```
UNITS [RET] [RET]
SALES $ [RET] [RET]
COST OF MATERIALS [RET] [RET]
GROSS MARGIN [RET] [RET]
GM AS % OF SALES [RET] [RET] [RET]

RENT [RET] [RET]
UTILITIES [RET] [RET]
SALARIES [RET] [RET]
TOTAL EXPENSES [RET] [RET]
EXP AS % OF SALES [RET] [RET] [RET]
```

Adding Rows To The Spreadsheet

When you reach the final spreadsheet line, Framework will not allow any more entries, since the spreadsheet was created with only 14 rows. To add more rows to the spreadsheet, follow these steps:

Select the Create Menu and highlight the selection,

Rows / Records: Add   {1}

Press [RET] and enter the number of rows to be added to the spreadsheet, in this case type "2".

Press [RET] to complete the operation. The spreadsheet now contains 16 rows. Move the cursor to cell A15 and complete the text entries as follows:

PROFIT [RET] [RET]
PROFIT AS % OF SALES [RET]

SPREAD1 Jan 1, 1980

	JAN	FEB	MAR	1ST QTR
UNITS	100	120	130	
SALES $	50000	58000	62000	
COST OF MATERIALS	25000	28000	30000	
GROSS MARGIN				
GM AS % OF SALES				
RENT	5000	5000	5000	
UTILITIES	2500	2600	2700	
SALARIES	10000	11000	12000	
TOTAL EXPENSES				
EXP AS % OF SALES				
PROFIT				
PROFIT AS % OF SALES				

Figure 5.1. Titles and data for SPREAD1.

Setting Column Width

Notice that the width of the first column must be wider to accommodate the longer titles. To change the size of a column, move the cursor to the column you wish to change and then use [F4 Size] key to change the width of the column. Follow these steps:

1. Move the highlight to the title "Profit as % of sales" (cell A16).
2. Press [F4 Size].
3. Press [→] (cursor right) 12 times.
4. Press [RET] to complete the operation. The highlight is now larger than the title.

Notice that the headings at the top of the page are aligned with the left side of the cells. The spreadsheet's appearance would be improved if these were centered over the columns.

To center the top row of titles over each column, follow these steps:

1. Locate the cursor on the cell B1 JAN.
2. Press [F6 Extend Select].
3. Press [TAB] three times to extend the highlight to cells C1, D1, and E1.
4. Select the Numbers Menu by pressing [CTRL] N.
5. Choose the Middle toggle by pressing the M key. The headings should now be centered over their respective columns.

Entering Data

It is very simple to enter data in a spreadsheet. To enter the data in SPREAD1, move the cursor to cell B3 (JAN/UNITS) and type the following entries (Press [Num Lock] if you wish to enter the data with the numeric keypad.):

```
100 [RET] [RET]
50000 [RET] [RET]
25000 [RET] [RET]
```

Press [RET] three more times to move the cursor down to cell B9 (JAN/RENT), then type:

```
5000  [RET] [RET]
2500  [RET] [RET]
10000 [RET] [RET]
```

Refer to figure 5.1 and enter the remaining data for FEB and MAR. Upon completion your spreadsheet should resemble that shown in figure 5.1. To toggle the numeric keypad back to cursor control, use the [Num Lock] key.

In the preceding sections of this chapter you have entered both numeric text and data. The titles (text) were automatically aligned left and the numeric entries were automatically aligned right. Remember that we changed the column titles to center alignment by using [F6 Extend Select] and the Numbers Menu.

The Numbers Menu contains four selections relating to alignment of cell entries. These are:

— Words Left / #s Right
— Left
— Right
— Middle

If these toggles are set on from the frame border, the global settings are changed, and all subsequent entries in the frame will be affected by the setting. If one of these toggles is set on after selecting specific cells within the frame, then only those cells selected will be affected. The default value for cell alignment is "Words Left / #s Right".

Printing The Spreadsheet

Before printing the spreadsheet, enter a header by moving the cursor to the frame border and pressing [F2 Edit Formula]. Type the following header:

@hc("SPREAD1 "&@DATE1(@TODAY)) [RET]

Now choose the Print Menu and print the spreadsheet. The printed output should appear as shown in figure 5.1.

Entering Formulas

All of the necessary data has been entered in the spreadsheet. The remaining values in the spreadsheet will be calculated using formulas. For example, the number of units for the first quarter is the sum of the units from Jan, Feb, and Mar.

To enter a cell formula, simply press [F2 Edit Formula]. Type the formula and press [RET] to complete the entry. It is not necessary to use [F2 Edit Formula] if you start the entry with one of the following symbols:

@ # $ (+ - " .

To enter the formula for the first quarter / units, move the cursor to cell E3 and type:

@sum(b3:d3) [RET]

Notice that the formula now appears in the left side of the status line and the value computed by the formula, "350", is displayed in cell E3.

Copying Formulas

Most spreadsheet applications include formulas which are used many times in the same document. For instance in column E, the total for the first quarter will be computed by summing the values for the first three months.

Framework allows you to copy formulas, automatically adjusting the cell references to account for the new position of the formula. We can copy the formula in E3 (1st Qtr/ units) to cell E4 (1st Qtr/ sales) and Framework will automatically change the formula from @sum(B3:D3) to @sum(B4:D4).

To copy the formula as described in the previous paragraph, follow these steps:

1. Highlight cell E3.
2. Press [F8 Copy].
3. Move the highlight to cell E4.
4. Press [RET] to complete the copy.

Notice that the new formula "@sum(b4:d4)" now appears in the status line and the value "170000" is displayed in E4.

Now use these same procedures to copy the formula from E4 to E5 by moving the cursor to E4 and pressing:

[F8 COPY] [↓]   [RET]

It is also possible to copy a range of cells all at once using the [F6 Extend Select] key.

To copy formulas from the range of cells E3:E5 to the new range of cells E9:E11, follow these steps:

1. Highlight cell E3.
2. Press [F6 Extend Select].
3. Press [↓] (cursor down) twice to move the cursor down to E5 which highlights cells E3 to E5.
4. Press [F8 Copy].
5. Move the cursor down to cell E9 and press [RET] to end the Copy operation.

The calculated values for E9 to E11 should appear on the screen.

Referencing Cells

In the formula for the 1st Qtr/ Units, cells B3 to D3 were referenced to calculate the formula in E3. These are known as relative references. A relative cell reference will be automatically adjusted by Framework when a formula or a cell reference is copied.

To illustrate, if cell E3 references the cell to its immediate left (D3), when the contents of cell E3 are copied to cell E4, the formula in E4 will reference the cell to its immediate left (D4).

Cell references may also be absolute. To specify an absolute cell reference use the $ symbol just before the cell column or row. The cell reference D3 will be copied to another cell as D3 (unchanged).

Cell references may also be mixed (absolute and relative), such as $D3 or D$3. If cell E3 references the cell $D3, when the contents of E3 are copied to cell F4, the formula in F4 would reference the cell $D4. If the cell E3 references the cell D$3, when the contents of E3 are copied to cell F4, the formula in F4 would reference the cell E$3.

Cell Coordinates

Cells can be referenced by three different methods. In the examples above, cell coordinates (E3, B3, etc.) were used to identify the position of the cells in the spreadsheet. Cells may also be identified by the column and row titles. This is known as **english language referencing**.

English language references can be displayed with the "!" ([Shift][1]) toggle. The identification of the current cell in the spreadsheet is displayed in the center of the status line at the bottom of the screen. To change the coordinates from and to the english language reference, use "!" as a toggle. Watch the center of the status line to see the effect of the "!" toggle.

To enter a formula using the english language references, follow these steps:

1. Move the cursor to the cell corresponding to Jan/-Gross Margin (B6) and press [!] (Shift-1) to toggle the english language references.
2. Press [F2 Formula Edit].
3. Press the [↑] (Cursor Up) key to invoke the cursor pointing mode.
4. Use the [↑] (Cursor Up) key to move the cursor to Jan/Sales $ and press [-] (Minus).
5. Use the [↓] (Cursor Down) key to move the cursor to Jan/Cost of Materials and press [RET].

The formula below the status line should appear as follows:

JAN.[SALES $] - JAN.COST OF MATERIALS

6. Press [RET] again to complete the entry and display the value "25000" in cell B6.
7. Use [!] to toggle back to cell coordinate referencing.

Cursor Pointing

In the previous example, the cell formula was created by cursor pointing. This is an efficient method of cell referencing since it eliminates many keyboard entry errors by visually selecting the correct cells.

Again, use cursor pointing to enter the formula for GM As % of Sales in cell B7. Follow these steps:

1. Move the cursor to cell B7 and press [F2 Formula Edit].
2. Use the [↑] (Cursor Up) key to invoke cursor pointing.
3. Use the [↑] (Cursor Up) key to move the cursor to cell B6 and type [/] (Division Sign).
4. Use the [↑] (Cursor Up) key to move the cursor to cell B4 (Sales $) and press [RET] twice.

The formula should now read as follows:

B6/B4

The value of the cell Jan/GM as % of sales should be .50.

Displaying a Percent

The calculated value of Jan/GM as % of sales was displayed as 0.5. To change this to a % display use the Numbers Menu as follows:

1. Use the cursor to select the cell B7.
2. Select the Numbers Menu and highlight the Percent selection.
3. Press [RET] to end the styling operation.

The value should now read 50.00%.

Completing The Spreadsheet

Complete the spreadsheet by entering formulas and copying formulas as follows:

1. Move the cursor to cell B12 and enter this formula:

@sum(B9:B11) [RET]

2. Move the cursor to cell B13 and enter this formula:

[F2 Formula Edit] B12/B4

3. With the cursor still in cell B13, style the cell by selecting the Numbers Menu and choosing Percent.
4. Move the cursor to cell B15 and enter this formula:

+B6-B12

The + sign is another arithmetic symbol which starts a formula entry.

    5. Move the cursor to cell B16 and enter this formula:

$$+B15/B4$$

    6. With the cursor still in cell B16, style the cell by selecting the Numbers Menu and choosing Percent.

    7. Move the cursor to B6 and press [F6 Extend Select] then use [↓] to extend the highlight to B7. Now type:

[F8 Copy] [→] [RET]

This copies the formulas from cell range B6:B7 to C6:C7. Repeat these keystrokes twice to copy formulas to cell ranges D6:D7 and E6:E7.

    8. Move the cursor to B12 and press [F6 Extend Select]. Then use [↓] 4 times to extend the highlight down to B16. Now type:

[F8 Copy] [→] [RET]

This copies the formulas from cell range B12:B15 to C12:C15. Repeat these keystrokes twice to copy formulas to cell ranges D12:D15 and E12:E15.

The spreadsheet should now appear as shown in figure 5.2.

SPREAD1   Jan 1, 1980

	JAN	FEB	MAR	1ST QTR
UNITS	100	120	130	350
SALES $	50000	58000	62000	170000
COST OF MATERIALS	25000	28000	30000	83000
GROSS MARGIN	25000	30000	32000	87000
GM AS % OF SALES	50.00%	51.72%	51.61%	51.18%
RENT	5000	5000	5000	15000
UTILITIES	2500	2600	2700	7800
SALARIES	10000	11000	12000	33000
TOTAL EXPENSES	17500	18600	19700	55800
EXP AS % OF SALES	35.00%	32.07%	31.77%	32.82%
PROFIT	7500	11400	12300	31200
PROFIT AS % OF SALES	15.00%	19.66%	19.84%	18.35%

Figure 5.2.   Complete spreadsheet, SPREAD1

Inserting and Deleting Columns and Rows

Columns or rows may be inserted into or deleted from a spreadsheet frame.

INSERTING ROWS AND COLUMNS

To insert rows into the spreadsheet, follow these steps:

1. Position the cursor in the row above the location of the rows to be added.

2. Select the Create Menu.

3. Select "Rows / Records: Add   {1}" by pressing [RET].

4. Type the number of rows to be added and press [RET].

The additional rows will be inserted into the spreadsheet immediately below the position of the cursor.

To insert columns into the spreadsheet, follow these steps:

1. Position the cursor in the column just before the position of the columns to be inserted.

2. Select the Create Menu.

3. Select "Columns/Fields: Add   {1}" by pressing [RET].

4. Enter the number of columns to be added and press [RET].

The additional columns will be inserted into the spreadsheet immediately to the right of the position of the cursor.

If you are inserting a single row or column, step 4 will consist of pressing [RET].

DELETING ROWS AND COLUMNS

To delete unwanted rows in a spreadsheet, follow these steps:

1. Position the cursor in the row to be deleted. (Use [F6 Extend Select] if you wish to delete a range of rows.)

2. Select the Edit Menu.

3. Select "Rows / Records: Remove" by pressing R.

4. Framework will beep and display the following warning:

NOT UNDOABLE: Continue Operation (y/n)?

Type "Y" to delete the indicated rows.

To delete unwanted columns in a spreadsheet, follow these steps:

1. Position the cursor in the column to be deleted. (Use [F6 Extend Select] if you wish to delete a range of columns.)

2. Select the Edit Menu.

3. Select "Columns/Fields: Remove" by pressing C.

4. Framework will beep and display the following warning:

   NOT UNDOABLE: Continue Operation (y/n)?

Type "Y" to delete the indicated columns.

Styling Entries

Entries in a spreadsheet may be styled to enhance the appearance of the document and improve readability. To illustrate styling follow these steps:

1. Bring the spreadsheet SPREAD1 to the desktop and relabel it SPREAD2.

2. Insert a row after UNITS. This will separate the row of data containing the number of units from the rows containing dollar amounts.

3. Move the cursor to cell B5 (JAN.SALES), press [F6 Extend Select] and press [→] (cursor right) three times to include the next three columns.

4. Now select the Numbers Menu and choose the "Currency" toggle. This will add the "$" sign, commas, and two decimals to the four fields containing sales dollars.

After performing step four you will find the fields are now filled with "*********." The additional characters use more space than is available in these columns.

To conserve space, change the number of decimal places to 0. To do this use [Uplevel] to move the cursor to the frame border, select the Numbers Menu and choose "Decimal Places {2} by pressing D. Then type "0" to change the number of decimal places to zero. Press [RET] to complete the operation. Reenter the frame by pressing [DOWNLEVEL].

5. With the cursor highlighting B5:E5, use the [↓] (cursor down) key to move the extended highlight down to the next row B6:E6 (COST OF MATERIALS). Press [F6 Extend Select] and the [↓] (cursor down) key to extend the highlight to the next row B7:E7 (GROSS MARGIN). The highlight should now be covering B6:E7.

6. Select the Numbers Menu and choose the "— Business" toggle to style the numbers included in the range B6:E7.

7. Move the cursor down to the next row (GM AS % OF SALES), and change the number of decimal places to "1" using the Numbers Menu.

Using the techniques illustrated above, style the rest of the spreadsheet to match the spreadsheet in figure 5.3.

The Numbers Menu

The Numbers Menu contains the styling selections for numeric data. Figure 5.4 illustrates the effect of each style.

SPREAD1   Jan 1, 1980

	JAN	FEB	MAR	1ST QTR
UNITS	100	120	130	350
SALES $	$50,000	$58,000	$62,000	$170,000
COST OF MATERIALS	25,000	28,000	30,000	83,000
GROSS MARGIN	25,000	30,000	32,000	87,000
GM AS % OF SALES	50.0%	51.7%	51.6%	51.2%
RENT	$5,000	$5,000	$5,000	$15,000
UTILITIES	2,500	2,600	2,700	7,800
SALARIES	10,000	11,000	12,000	33,000
TOTAL EXPENSES	17,500	18,600	19,700	55,800
EXP AS % OF SALES	35.0%	32.1%	31.8%	32.8%
PROFIT	$7,500	$11,400	$12,300	$31,200
PROFIT AS % OF SALES	15.0%	19.7%	19.8%	18.4%

Figure 5.3.   SPREAD2 spreadsheet with styled entries.

STYLING WITH THE NUMBERS MENU

General	98765.43	98765.4321	98765.
Decimal Places ()	2	4	0
Integer	98765	98765	98765
Fixed Decimal	98765.43	98765.4321	98765.
Currency	$98,765.43	$98,765.4321	$98,765
Business	98,765.43	98,765.4321	98,765
Percent	9876543.21%	9876543.2100%	9876543%
Scientific	9.88E+4	9.8765E+4	1.E+5

Figure 5.4.   Styling with the Numbers Menu

Advanced Spreadsheet Features

The following are some advanced spreadsheet features. Some of these are covered in more detail in chapter 9 (see FRED Programming Language, chapter 9).

PROTECT FROM EDITING

You may wish to use the same spreadsheet for several documents. For instance, SPREAD2 could be used for each of the four quarters of the year. All you need to do is erase the variable input data and reenter the data for the new quarter.

To facilitate this kind of use, Framework provides a "protect from editing" / "allow editing" feature in the Edit Menu. To illustrate these features, follow these steps:

1. Display the spreadsheet SPREAD2 on the desktop.
2. With the cursor in the frame border of SPREAD2, select the Edit Menu and choose the "— Protect from Editing" toggle.
3. Now use [Downlevel] to enter the frame and highlight the data range B3:D6 using [F6 Extend Select] and the appropriate cursor movement keys.
4. Select the Edit Menu and choose "Allow Editing."
5. Now highlight the range B10:D12 and choose "Allow Editing" to unprotect this range.
6. To blank these cells to allow a new set of data to be entered, move the cursor to the frame border and choose "Blank All" from the Frames Menu.

All unprotected cells in the frame are blanked and ready to receive new data. The cells remain formatted (styled) so that the new data will appear in the same style as the previous data. Those protected cells which contain formulas will continue to display the previously calculated data until the spreadsheet is recalculated.

Referencing Other Spreadsheets

One of Framework's powerful features is its ability to reference other spreadsheet frames. This means that you can use the input from one spreadsheet in another as long as the other spreadsheet is on the desktop.

As an example, suppose that you had created another spreadsheet, SPREAD3, and you wanted to enter the first quarter profit from the spreadsheet, SPREAD2. The references to be used would be as follows:

SPREAD2.E16

The reference must include the path to the frame, the frame name and the specific cell or cell range, separated by periods (.). *See* Reference Look Up Rules, FRED Programming Language, chapter 9.

Creating Keyboard Macros

Keyboard macros are used to store a series of keystrokes that can be recalled by pressing one key in combination with the [Alt] key. As an example, one operation that is frequently performed in a spreadsheet is the use of the copy operation to copy from one cell (or range of cells) to the cell (or range of cells) just to the right.

Let's create a keyboard macro which performs the copy operation. The Framework Utilities disk includes the MAC-LIB.FW file which can be used to store all of your keyboard macros.

Follow these steps to create a keyboard macro in the MACLIB.FW file:

1. Insert the Framework Utilities disk in a disk drive.

2. Load the MACLIB.FW file onto the desktop.

3. Press F5-Recalc.

4. Press [ALT]-F2 and the following prompt appears:

Type [ALT]-key to associate with the macro

The keyboard macro [ALT]-F2 is provided with Framework. It facilitates the process of entering keyboard macros.

5. You may chose any of the fourty-six [ALT]-key combinations except [ALT]-F2 of course. Press [ALT]-C as the macro key for the copy macro.

6. Simply enter the keystrokes to be performed by the macro just as you would during execution.

[F8-Copy]   [→]   [RET]

7. End the macro definition process by pressing the [ALT]-key combination a second time, [ALT]-C.

The macro is now stored. To use the macro, move the cursor to the cell or cells to be copied and press [ALT]-C. The contents of the cell will be copied to the next cell to the right.

To view and or edit the macro, open the file MACLIB and press [Downlevel]. Highlight the frame for the Alt key, in this case "C" and press [F2 Formula Edit]. You may edit the formula just as you would any other formula. *See* Keyboard Macros, FRED Programming Language, chapter 9.

Arithmetic and Relational Operators

Arithmetic and relational operators are described in chapter 9. *See* Operators, FRED Programming Language, chapter 9.

Functions

Refer to the Framework Reference Manual for a list of functions. *See* FRED Language Functions by Class in chapter 11 of the Framework Reference Manual.

6

Data Base

If you have never used a computerized data base management system before, the concept of a data base and how it is managed may be a bit puzzling. The fact is everyone practices manual data base management at some time in a manner quite similar to its computerized counterpart.

If you maintain an address book, either in the home or at the office, you are practicing data base management. Each name and the associated address, phone number, etc. are data. All of the names and addresses are considered a data base or group of related information. You are performing data base management when you perform this type of organized record keeping.

A computerized data base system functions with the same basic principles used in a manual record keeping system. However, a computerized data base system allows complete data management tasks to be performed in a fraction of the time that would be required with a manual system.

Components of a Data Base

A simple example should make the concept of data base management more clear. Figure 6.1 shows a simple customer list which keeps track of the customer base including the name, address, phone number and other pertinent information.

```
NAME           STREET          CITY          STATE ZIP   PHONE     CONTACT  SIZE
==================================================================================
DOWNTOWNER     957 EUCLID AVE  CLEVELAND     OH    44029 749-1299  HAL SHAW  38
ENGLISH PUB    14801 LAKESIDE  LAKEWOOD      OH    44106 226-8011  ANDERS    42
JOE'S PLACE    1492 BROADWAY   BEDFORD       OH    44118 439-1954  SMITH     24
CHEERS         18042 CEDAR     BEACHWOOD     OH    44122 752-8751  COLSON    85
SOLOMAN'S      1298 LARKWOOD   MENTOR        OH    44078 567-3298  JONES     27
```

Figure 6.1. Customer Data Base

Across the top of the table, each of the eight pieces of information which are of interest (customer name, address, etc.) are known as **fields**. When taken as a group for a specific customer, these eight fields make up a **record**. The entire table, taken as a whole, will be contained in a **frame**.

These three concepts, **field, record** and **frame**, provide the basis for how data base information is stored and manipulated in Framework.

Creating a Data Base

Before you set up a data base in Framework, you should thoroughly consider the type of information it will manage.

One of your first decisions is to determine the number of fields each record will contain. Each record will be limited to the number of fields defined in the data base frame. Therefore, you must define an adequate number of fields to satisfy every record to be added to the data base. The data base can be changed at any time, but starting with the correct data base design saves time.

The number of records which a data base can store is determined by the amount of "RAM" memory installed in your computer. The data base must be designed to be small enough to fit into your computer's memory. You can limit the size of your data base by reducing the size and/or number of fields. Doing so will enable the data base to hold more records, since each smaller record requires less memory.

Once you determine the structure of your data base, creating the data base frame will be relatively simple if you are already familiar with spreadsheet frames. Simply select the Create menu and edit the Width and Height options to match the number of data base fields and records, respectively. The Width and Height options default to a fourteen field and fourteen record data base. Next you select the Database option and Framework will create an empty data base frame.

As with any other frame, the first step in using a data base frame is to enter its label. Type in the frame label and press [RET].

Press [DOWNLEVEL] to move inside the data base frame. The screen cursor will appear just above the double horizontal lines in the upper left hand corner of the frame. The field names can now be entered from left to right.

Figure 6.2. Empty data base frame

Let's create a Framework data base for the customer information which appeared in figure 6.1.

1. Select the Create menu and edit the Width option to equal eight.

2. Select the Database option and the empty data base frame appears on the screen.

3. Type in CUSTOMER as the frame name and press [RET].

4. Enter the CUSTOMER frame by pressing the [DOWN-LEVEL] key and type in the first field, NAME.

5. Press the [TAB] key to advance to the next field location and type in the next field label, STREET, followed by the [TAB] key.

6. Enter the remaining six fields by typing in the following:

```
CITY [TAB]
STATE [TAB]
ZIP [TAB]
PHONE [TAB]
CONTACT [TAB]
SIZE [TAB]
```

NAME	STREET	CITY	STATE	ZIP	PHONE	CONTACT	SIZE

Figure 6.3. Customer data base

The newly created data base should appear as in figure 6.3. The field names are positioned above the double line. The work area below the double line is available for entry of data base records.

Entering Data Base Records

Entering records in a data base parallels the process of entering data in a spreadsheet frame. The cursor movement keys function in an identical manner in both the spreadsheet and data base frames (see table 5.1).

Let's enter a data base record to illustrate the similarity. Follow these steps to enter data base records:

1. Press the [HOME] key to return to the first field.
2. Press [RET] to move down to the next record.
3. Type in the data, in this case DOWNTOWNER, and press the [TAB] key to advance to the next field.

Complete this record by entering the remaining fields:

[SPACE BAR] 957 EUCLID AVE [TAB]
CLEVELAND [TAB]
OH [TAB]
[SPACE BAR] 44029 [TAB]
[SPACE BAR] 749-1299 [TAB]
HAL SHAW [TAB]
38 [TAB]

Just as in a spreadsheet frame, when you enter a text character field which begins with a number, you must tell Framework that the field is text by pressing the [SPACE BAR].

Enter the remaining data base records shown in figure 6.4 by following the steps outlined above.

Field Lengths

You have probably noticed that the data entered into the first three fields, NAME, STREET and CITY, does not fit into the default field width of nine characters. Each individual field should be adjusted to conform to the width of data being entered. If the default width is larger than required, it should be reduced to conserve memory.

```
╔═[CUSTOMER]════════════════════════════════════╗

 NAME         STREET       CITY      STATE ZIP  PHONE     CONTACT  SIZE

 DOWNTOWNER   957 EUCLID AVE CLEVELAND   OH   44029 749-1299 HAL SHAW  38
 ENGLISH PUB  14801 LAKESIDE LAKEWOOD    OH   44106 226-8011 ANDERS    42
 JOE'S PLACE  1492 BROADWAY  BEDFORD     OH   44118 439-1954 SMITH     24
 CHEERS       18042 CEDAR    BEACHWOOD   OH   44122 752-8751 COLSON    85
 SOLOMAN'S    1298 LARKWOOD  MENTOR      OH   44078 567-3298 JONES     27

╚═══════════════════════════════════════════════╝
```

Figure 6.4. Customer data base updated with records

To change a field width use the following steps:

1. Locate the screen cursor anywhere in the field (column).

2. Press the [F4-Size] key.

3. Press the Right arrow key to increase the field width and the Left arrow key to decrease the field width.

4. Press the [RET] key when the field width reaches the proper size.

To change the Name field, press the [HOME] key to locate the screen cursor in this field. Press the [F4-Size] key and use the Right arrow [→] key to increase the field width by six characters. Note, the field width is displayed in the lower right-hand corner of the screen display. When the field width reaches fifteen, press [RET] to accept the new field width.

Modifying a Data Base

A data base will often evolve to suit a particular application. As the application changes, the data base can also be changed when necessary. Generally, a data base can be changed to suit the application by deleting or adding data base fields.

ADDING DATA BASE FIELDS

The same steps are used to add a field to a data base as those used to add a column in a spreadsheet frame. Let's add a field for comments to the Customer data base.

1. Highlight the field which should appear to the left of the new field, in this case SIZE.
2. Select the Create menu by pressing the [INS] key or [CTRL]-C.
3. Press C to select the Columns/Fields:Add option.
4. The default value of 1 appears. Change this value by typing in the desired number of fields to be added.
5. Press [RET] to add the field(s).

A blank field will appear to the right of the SIZE field. Move the screen cursor to the new field and enter its field label, COMMENTS. By pressing the [F4-Size] key, the field width can be increased to twenty characters.

REMOVING DATA BASE FIELDS

If you find that your data base contains information which is not being used, the fields which contain the information should be deleted. Not only will this save time when entering data base records, it will conserve memory which allows more records in the data base.

Follow these steps to delete a field:

1. Locate the screen cursor at the field to be removed.
2. Select the Edit menu by pressing the [INS] key or entering [CTRL]-E.
3. Press C to select the Column/Fields: Remove option.
4. Framework will display the message:

    NOT UNDOABLE: Continue Operation (y/n)

    to alert you that the field and its contents can not be recovered.
5. Enter Y to remove the field from the data base.

To conserve memory in the Customer data base, delete the COMMENTS field from the data base using the procedure outlined above.

Manipulating the Data Base

The advantage of creating a data base on Framework is that the program offers powerful functions which allow you to access and manipulate data. These functions not only significantly speed data management operations, they also allow operations not feasible with a manual system.

SORTING

Many applications require information to be arranged in a particular order. In a data base frame the records can be rearranged by sorting.

Follow these steps to reorder a data base frame.

1. Locate the screen cursor anywhere in the field to be used as the basis for the sort.
2. Select the Locate menu by entering [CTRL]-L.
3. Select the Ascending Sort option by pressing the A key. The data base records will be ordered in alphabetical or numeric order based on the data in the selected field.

Or;

Select the Descending Sort option by pressing the D
key. The data base records will be ordered in reverse
alphabetical or numeric order based on the data in the
selected field.

If you locate the screen cursor in the NAME field of the
Customer data base and select the Locate menu, the data base
records can be rearranged in alphabetical order by selecting the
Ascending Sort option.

[CUSTOMER]

NAME	STREET	CITY	STATE	ZIP	PHONE	CONTACT	SIZE
CHEERS	18042 CEDAR	BEACHWOOD	OH	44122	752-8751	COLSON	85
DOWNTOWNER	957 EUCLID AVE	CLEVELAND	OH	44029	749-1299	HAL SHAW	38
ENGLISH PUB	14801 LAKESIDE	LAKEWOOD	OH	44106	226-8011	ANDERS	42
JOE'S PLACE	1492 BROADWAY	BEDFORD	OH	44118	439-1954	SMITH	24
SOLOMAN S	1298 LARKWOOD	MENTOR	OH	44079	567-3298	JONES	27

Figure 6.5. Customer data base sorted alphabetically on the
NAME field

In some instances, you may want to arrange records by
more than one field. For example, if you maintained a phone
directory with the fields LASTNAME and FIRSTNAME it
could be sorted alphabetically on the LASTNAME field.

However, if there are records with identical LASTNAME entries, a further rearrangement based on the FIRSTNAME field may be desired.

A data base frame can be sorted based on more than one field. However, Framework is limited to sorting one field during each sort operation. To sort on multiple fields you begin by sorting the least significant field. After the first sort operation is complete, the data base is sorted by the next least significant field. This process if repeated until the most significant field is sorted.

SEARCHING FOR RECORDS

A data base frame can be searched for numeric or text data just as you seached a word frame. There are two rules to keep in mind about cursor placement:

- Place the cursor in the frame border to search the entire data base.
- Place the cursor in a field to limit the search to that specific field.

Once you position the screen cursor, select the Locate menu by pressing [CTRL]-L. Press the S key to select the Search option and type in the characters to be found. The Replace option can also be used if any entries require revision.

Follow these steps to search for all cities beginning with the letter B in the Customer data base:

1. Position the screen cursor in the CITY field.
2. Select the LOCATE menu by entering [CTRL]-L.
3. Press the S key to search the data base and type in the character string to be found, B.

4. Press the [RET] key and the screen cursor moves to the first field entry which matches the search criteria, BEACHWOOD.

5. Press the Down Arrow key to locate the next field entry which satisfies the search criteria, BEDFORD.

SELECTING DATA BASE RECORDS

Framework can use all of the functions available in the FRED language as selection criteria for data base frames. By entering **filtering formulas** in the data base frame label, Framework removes the records which do not meet the criteria leaving only the records which satisfy the formula in the frame label.

The filtering of records from the screen can be overridden by selecting the Frames menu and entering the O key to select the Open All option. All of the data base records will again display on the screen, however the order of the records will now be changed. The records which satisfy the selection criteria will appear at the top of the screen display followed by those records which do not meet the criteria.

To enter a filtering formula, first select a data base frame. With the cursor on the frame label, follow these steps:

1. Press the [F2-Edit Formula] key.
2. Enter the selection formula.
3. Press [RET] to invoke the formula.

Let's enter a few example filtering formulas to illustrate their use. With the cursor on the frame label of the Customer data base frame, type in the following:

```
[F2-Edit Formula]
CITY = "CLEVELAND"
[RET]
```

The screen display will change so that it appears as in figure 6.6.

```
╔═[CUSTOMER]══════════════════════════════════════╗
║                                                  ║
║ NAME         STREET       CITY       STATE ZIP   PHONE    CONTACT  SIZE ║
║                                                  ║
║ DOWNTOWNER   957 EUCLID AVE CLEVELAND  OH   44029 749-1299 HAL SHAW  38  ║
║                                                  ║
║                                                  ║
║                                                  ║
║                                                  ║
║                                                  ║
║                                                  ║
║                                                  ║
║                                                  ║
║                                                  ║
╚══════════════════════════════════════════════════╝
```

Figure 6.6.   Filtering the Customer data base for the CITY
Cleveland

Press the [UPLEVEL] key to return the cursor to the
frame label and enter another filtering formula.

```
[F2-Edit Formula]
ZIP > "44099"
[RET]
```

The three records with a ZIP above "44099" will be displayed on the screen (see figure 6.7). If you print the data base,
only these three records will be printed.

```
╔═[CUSTOMER]════════════════════════════════════════════╗
║                                                        ║
║  NAME        STREET        CITY        STATE ZIP   PHONE     CONTACT  SIZE  ║
║  ─────────────────────────────────────────────────────────────────        ║
║  CHEERS      18042 CEDAR    BEACHWOOD    OH    44122 752-8751 COLSON   85   ║
║  ENGLISH PUB 14801 LAKESIDE LAKEWOOD     OH    44106 226-8011 ANDERS   42   ║
║  JOE'S PLACE 1492 BROADWAY  BEDFORD      OH    44118 439-1954 SMITH    24   ║
║                                                        ║
║                                                        ║
╚════════════════════════════════════════════════════════╝
```

Figure 6.7. Filtering formula for the ZIP field limiting the data base to entries above "44099"

If you need to examine the entire data base, select the Frames menu. Press the O key to select the Open All option, and the remainder of the records will appear on the screen.

While these simple examples illustrate the function of a filter formula, they don't fully illustrate the power of the command. Using the built-in functions as well as your own user defined functions, a data base frame can be manipulated to accomplish virtually any information need. For example, the @and function can be used to combine two or more formulas into multiple selection criteria.

```
[CUSTOMER]

NAME          STREET       CITY         STATE ZIP    PHONE     CONTACT  SIZE

CHEERS        18042 CEDAR    BEACHWOOD    OH    44122 752-8751 COLSON    85
ENGLISH PUB   14801 LAKESIDE LAKEWOOD     OH    44106 226-8011 ANDERS    42
JOE'S PLACE   1492 BROADWAY  BEDFORD      OH    44118 439-1954 SMITH     24
DOWNTOWNER    957 EUCLID AVE CLEVELAND    OH    44029 749-1299 HAL SHAW  38
SOLOMAN'S     1298 LARKWOOD  MENTOR       OH    44078 567-3298 JONES     27
```

Figure 6.8. Using the Open All option with a filtering formula

Data Base Forms

The [F10-View] key is normally used to switch to outline view of frames. The only exception is with data base frames. When you press [F10] from inside a data base frame, the data base switches to what is referred to as "Forms View."

In forms view, each data base field is displayed as an individual frame. The data base appears on the screen as three columns of frames each labeled with a field label. Only one data base record is visible within the field frames.

To move through the data base while in the forms view, use the arrow keys located on the numeric keypad. Pressing the [→] key moves the cursor through the data base fields of one record. The cursor moves from left to right across the first row of fields and then advances to the following rows. When the cursor is in the last data base field, pressing the [→] key will cause the next data base record to appear on the form. To back-up through the data base, use the [←] key. To move through the data base one record at a time, use the [↑] and [↓] keys. The next or previous record will appear with the cursor in the same field.

ARRANGING THE FIELD FRAMES

The data base forms view is primarily used to arrange the data base records in the structure of a form for printing. The field frames can be moved and resized to your specifications.

To illustrate the forms concept, let's develop a mailing label form for the Customer data base. Bring the Customer frame onto the desktop and press the [DOWNLEVEL] key to move inside the frame. To display the Customer data base as a form, press the [F10-View] key.

```
┌═[CUSTOMER]══════════════════════════════════┐
║ ┌[NAME]═══┐   ┌[STREET]═══┐   ┌[CITY]═══┐ ║
║ │         │   │           │   │         │ ║
║ │         │   │           │   │         │ ║
║ └─────────┘   └───────────┘   └─────────┘ ║
║ ┌[STATE]══┐   ┌[ZIP]══════┐   ┌[PHONE]══┐ ║
║ │         │   │           │   │         │ ║
║ │         │   │           │   │         │ ║
║ └─────────┘   └───────────┘   └─────────┘ ║
║ ┌[CONTACT]┐   ┌[SIZE]═════┐   ┌[ ]══════┐ ║
║ │         │   │           │   │         │ ║
║ │         │   │           │   │         │ ║
║ └─────────┘   └───────────┘   └─────────┘ ║
└═════════════════════════════════════════════┘
```

Figure 6.9.   Customer data base in "Forms View"

The field frames can be moved and resized with the [F3-Drag] and [F4-Size] keys, respectively. The NAME field should remain in the upper right hand corner. Press the Right arrow [→] key to advance to the STREET field. Invoke the "Drag" mode by pressing the [F3-Drag] key. Use the Left arrow [←] key to move this frame in the upper right hand corner so that it covers the NAME field frame. Press the Down arrow [↓] key once and then [RET] to select this new frame position. Use the "Drag" mode to move the next field, CITY, into the upper right-hand corner covering the NAME field. Press the Down arrow [↓] key twice and then [RET] to select the frame position for the CITY field. Finally, the STATE and ZIP fields should be "Dragged" into position next to the CITY field as they appear in figure 6.10.

The first five field frames must also be resized to the appropriate field width. If you recall from earlier in this chapter, the NAME, STREET and CITY fields are fifteen charaters wide and the STATE and ZIP fields are six charaters wide. Each field frame should be adjusted to these widths using the [F4-Size] key. Refer to the previous example for instructions for sizing a field.

The last three fields should not appear on the data base form. To eliminate these fields, the frames which contain the three fields must be closed. These frames are closed just as any other frame. Simply move to the frame outline by pressing the Right arrow [→] key and press [RET]. The contents area of the frame will no longer display data base information. Close these three frames to complete the mailing label form.

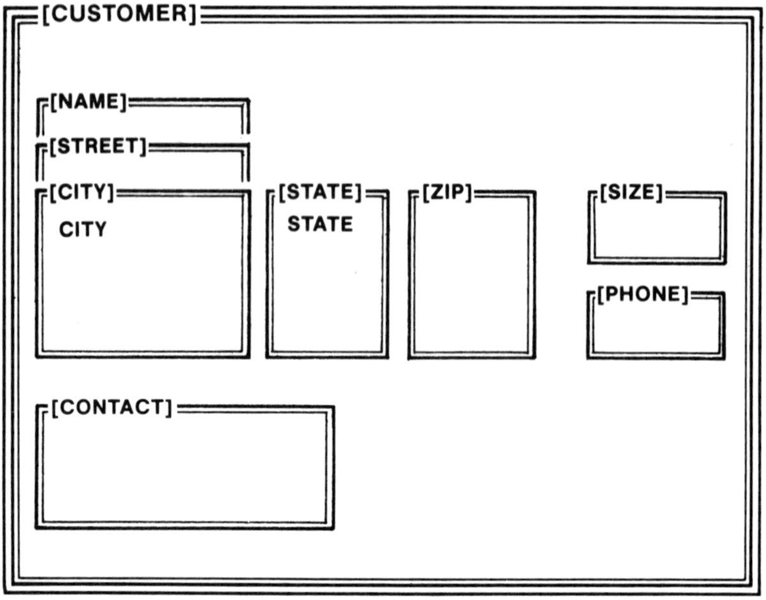

Figure 6.10. Customer Mailing Label Form

To print the data base form, move to the Customer frame outline by pressing the [UPLEVEL] key. Press the [INS] key and select the Print menu. Press the B key to begin printing the forms.

The forms which are printed have several problems. First, the frame labels for each field are printed. The other problem is the closed frames are also printed.

To eliminate these two items from the printed form, several Output Options must be changed in the Print menu. Use the [INS] key to access the Print menu and press the O key to display the various Output Options.

```
Begin on Page                          {1}
End after Page                      {9999}

Number of Copies                       {1}
--Skip Closed Frames
--Formulas Only
on Print Frame Labels
```

Figure 6.11. PRINT Menu Output Option

The Skip Closed Frames defaults to an "off" setting. Move the cursor so that this option is highlighted and press [RET] to set this option "on." Move the screen cursor to the last option, Print Frame Labels. This option is normally in the "on" position, but for this particular form we will disable the option by pressing [RET].

To reprint the mailing labels select the Begin option. An example of the printed labels appears in figure 6.12.

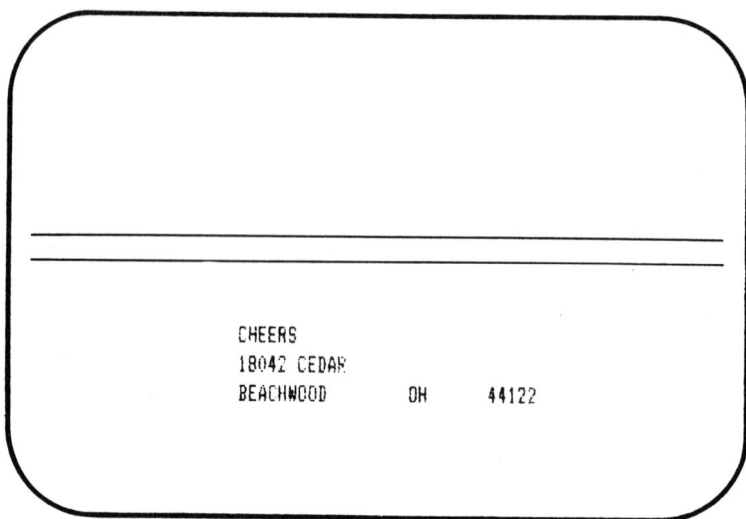

Figure 6.12. Customer Mailing Label

7

Graphics

In the preceding chapters we learned how to use Framework to process and keep track of information. In this chapter we will demonstrate how Framework's graphics feature can be used to display this information effectively.

We will use the spreadsheet depicted in figure 7.1 throughout our discussion. We recommend that you enter this data in a spreadsheet frame and save it on disk as GRAPHDAT.

```
┌[GRAPHDAT]════════════════════════════════════════════╗
║                                                        ║
║         A           B              C                   ║
║   1     Year        Gross          Net                 ║
║   2                 Income         Income              ║
║   3     1980             -10250         -7569          ║
║   4     1981              8400          6570           ║
║   5     1982             32860         20500           ║
║   6     1983             53700         40400           ║
║   7     1984             63090         45089           ║
║   8                                                    ║
║   9                                                    ║
║  10                                                    ║
║                                                        ║
║                                                        ║
║                                                        ║
║                                                        ║
║                                                        ║
║                                                        ║
╚════════════════════════════════════════════════════════╝
```

Figure 7.1. GRAPHDAT

Drawing a Simple Graph-Spreadsheet

Creating a graph in Framework is a simple process. Six fundamental steps are involved. Suppose the GRAPHDAT spreadsheet was displayed in its tray, and you wanted to create a bar graph of the net income from 1980 through 1984. You could create the graph by observing the following steps:

1. Press [DOWNLEVEL] to move the highlight into the frame body.

2. Use the cursor movement keys to position the highlight at cell C3.

3. Press [F6 Extend Select]. Press the Down arrow cursor movement key four times to extend the highlight to frame C7. Press [RET] to end the selection process.

4. Press Ctrl-G D. Or press INS; use the cursor movement keys to select the Graphs menu; and select the Draw New Graph option.

5. The following will be displayed in the message area:

Press RETURN to draw graph here, or select desired frame and press RETURN

If you press RETURN, a new frame will automatically be created to hold the graph. If you wish to place the new graph in an existing graph or empty word processing frame, you can do so by selecting that frame and pressing RETURN.

We'll assume that you want to create a new frame, so just press RETURN. The graph will be drawn in a new frame as shown in figure 7.2.*

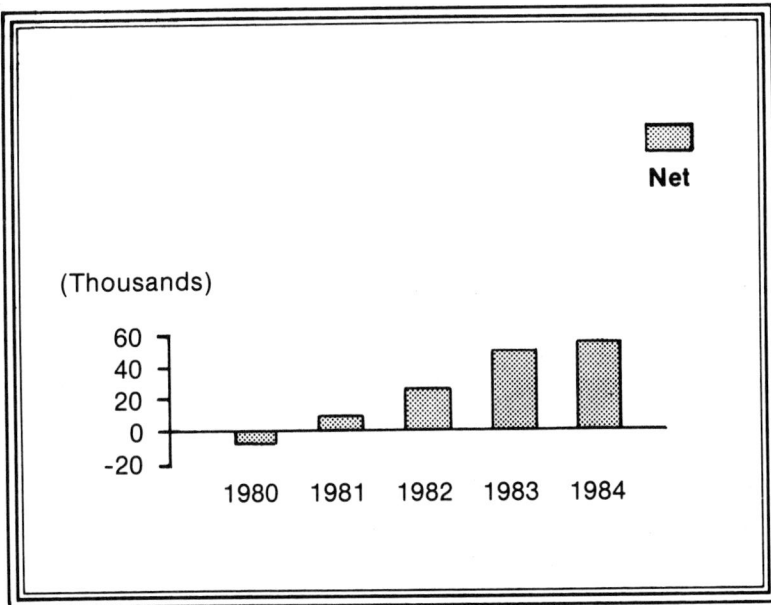

Figure 7.2. Netinc Graph

---

* If your graph's X-axis labels don't correspond to those shown in figure 7.2, don't be concerned. Graph labels are explained on page 156.

Notice that an empty tray was created along with the frame.

6. Neither the frame nor its corresponding tray have a name. Let's name our frame Netinc. Type in Netinc and press [RET].

Congratulations! If you entered the speadsheet depicted in figure 7.1 and followed these 6 steps, you have created your first Framework graph.

Drawing a Simple Graph-Data Base

The procedure for drawing a graph from a data base is almost identical to that for drawing a graph from a spreadsheet. With a data base, select the field or fields that you wish to graph. Keep in mind, however, that Framework graphs every record in the data base. If only selected records are to be included in the graph, the extraneous records must first be filtered. *See* chapter 6 for information on filtering.

Altering The Graph

Now that we've learned how to create a simple bar graph, let's experiment by altering our Netinc example.

CHANGE THE SIZE [F4 Size]

You can change the size of a graph frame by using the [F4-Size] key. Experiment by pressing [F4-Size]. Then press the Right arrow key twice followed by the Down arrow key. Press [RET] and the graph frame expands.

You can also drag, copy and move a graph frame as you would any other Framework frame by using [F3-Drag], [F7-Move], or [F8-Copy].

REDRAWING THE GRAPH [F5-Recalc]

Supposed we changed cell C3 of our spreadsheet so that it contained +7562 rather than -7562. When we subsequently redisplay the Netinc graph, it still displays 1980 net income as -7562.

We can change the graph so that it corresponds with the revised spreadsheet by pressing [F5-Recalc]. This key recalculates the data base or spreadsheet data used to draw the graph and then redraws the graph accordingly.

CHANGING THE GRAPH TITLE

Perhaps you already noticed that when we assigned our new graph frame the name Netinc, that same name was used as the graph title. Suppose we wanted to change our graph title to uppercase characters, NETINC. To do so move the highlight to the frame border and enter NETINC. Notice that the graph title remains Netinc. Press [F5-Recalc] and the graph title will change to NETINC.

You can also display your title in bold, italic or underlined. Position the highlight on the graph frame and follow the steps outlined below to display the graph title in italic:

1. Press the space bar to place the frame name in the edit line.

2. Press [F6-Extend Select] followed by the End key on the numeric keypad. NETINC is now highlighted on the edit line.

3. Press Ctrl-W I to select the Italic option from the Words menu. The frame name will appear in italic on both the frame border and the edit line.

4. Press [RET] [F5 Recalc], and Framework will redraw the graph with the title displayed in italic.

You can use any number of Words menu options to display the graph title. For example, you can choose bold, underline, bold italic, italic underline, or even bold italic underline.

LABELING THE GRAPH

Notice in figure 7.2 that the NETINC graph has a label for the X-axis (1980, 1981, etc.) as well as the Y-axis (-20, 0, 20, 40, 60). These were generated automatically when the graph was drawn.

Framework automatically labels the Y-axis with a number scale. Two options are available in the Graphs menu for listing the X-axis:

> Column has X-axis labels
> Row has X-axis labels

"Column has X-axis labels" labels the X-axis with the headings from the spreadsheet or data base's first column. "Row has X-axis labels" labels the X-axis with the headings from the spreadsheet or data base's first row.

In our NETINC example, we created a graph where the first column was used as the X-axis label. Now let's create a graph where the first row is used as the X-axis label.

1. Move the highlight to the border of GRAPHDAT. Press [DOWNLEVEL]. Position the highlight at B3 and press [F6-Extend Select]. Press the Right arrow key followed by [RET].

2. Press Ctrl-G to display the Graphs menu. Move the highlight to Row Has X-axis Labels and press [RET]. The "ON" toggle will be displayed next to Row Has X-axis Labels; it will simultaneously disappear from Column Has X-axis Labels.

3. Move the highlight to Draw New Graph and press [RET]. The following prompt will be displayed:

   Press RETURN to draw graph here, or
   select the desired frame and press RETURN

   The graph depicted in figure 7.3 will appear on your screen.

4. Label the new graph INC80.

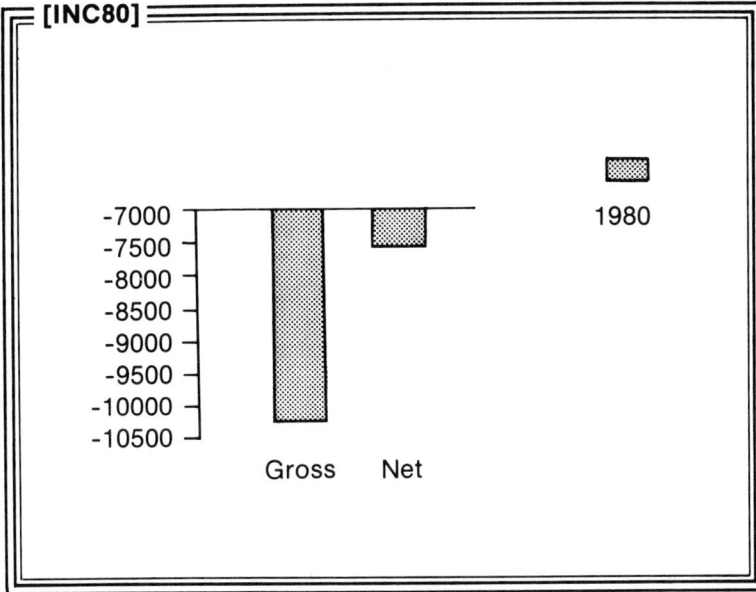

Figure 7.3. INC80 graph

Notice in INC80 that the row was used as the X-axis label.

Finally notice the information in the upper right-hand corner of both INC80 and NETINC. This is known as the graph legend. A graph legend explains the symbols used in printing the graph. Notice that when "Column has X-axis labels" was indicated for NETINC, the row was used for the legend. When "Row has X-axis labels" was specified for INC80, the column value appeared in the legend. Generally, one set of headings (row or column) is used for the legend and the other is used for the label.

GRAPHING SEVERAL COLUMNS OF DATA

Suppose we wished to modify our NETINC graph so that both the gross and net income figures were displayed. Follow the steps listed below to see how easily this can be accomplished using Framework:

1. Move the highlight to the border of GRAPHDAT.

2. Press [DOWNLEVEL] to move the highlight into the frame. Using the cursor movement keys, move the highlight to cell B3. Press [F6-Extend Select]. Press the Down arrow key 4 times and the Right arrow key once to extend the highlight over all of the income data. Press [RET] to end the selection.

3. Press Ctrl-G to display the Graphs menu. Make sure the toggle for Column Has X-axis Labels is "ON". Then select Draw New Graph. The following prompt will appear:

   Press RETURN to draw graph here, or
   select desired frame and press RETURN

4. Press [RET] to display the new graph as shown in figure 7.4. Notice how the gross and net income figures are displayed side-by-side using the different legends. Let's name our new graph NETINC2.

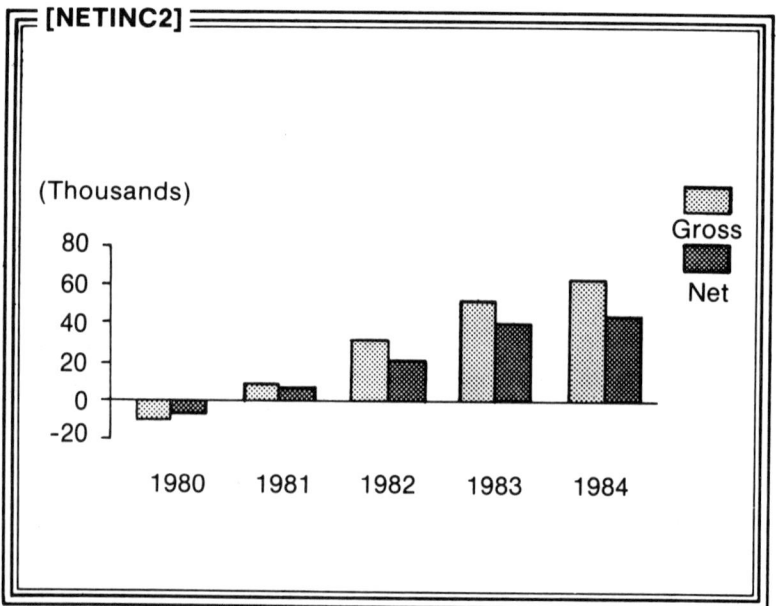

Figure 7.4.   NETINC2

COLOR MONITOR WITH GRAPHS

If your system includes a color monitor, you can display your graphs in color as well as black and white. Framework will initially display the graph in the high resolution mode which will appear as black and white on your screen. The graph will be displayed across the full screen in color by pressing [F9-Zoom]. Pressing this key once more causes Framework to redraw the graph in black and white at its normal size.

Other Graph Types

To this point we've worked strictly with bar graphs. Framework, however, also offers other types of graphs including:

Stacked Bar
Pie
Line
Marked Points
X-Y

We will examine each of these in the following sections.

STACKED BAR

A stacked bar graph resembles a bar graph with multiple columns, except that the bars are placed in a single vertical stack rather than side by side.

Follow the steps outlined in the section entitled "Graphing Several Columns of Data," except specify Stacked Bar rather than Bar in the Graphs menu. Note the error message:

Negative numbers aren't allowed in Stacked Bar graphs

Now try again using only the income data from 1981 through 1984. Your graph should resemble that shown in figure 7.5.

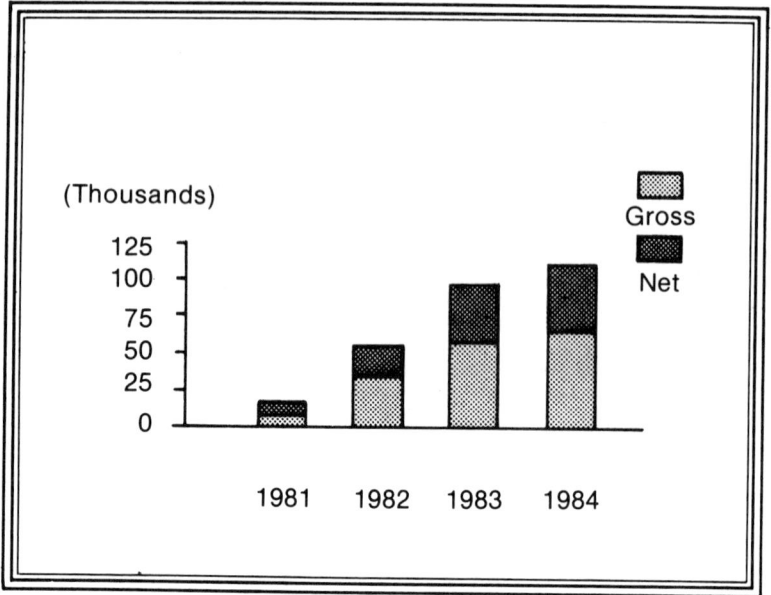

Figure 7.5.   Stacked bar graph

PIE

A pie graph depicts data as slices of a pie. Only a single row or column can be included in a pie graph. As with stacked bar graphs, negative values are not allowed in pie graphs.

You should be able to create a pie graph depicting net income from 1981 through 1984. Give it a try. Your graph should resemble that shown in figure 7.6

LINE GRAPH

A line graph depicts data as a set of coordinates with a connecting line. The line may not appear on a non-graphics monitor. Try displaying 1981 through 1984 net income as a line graph. Your graph should resemble that shown in figure 7.7.

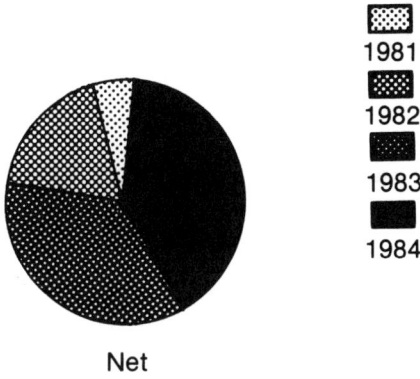

Figure 7.6.   Pie graph

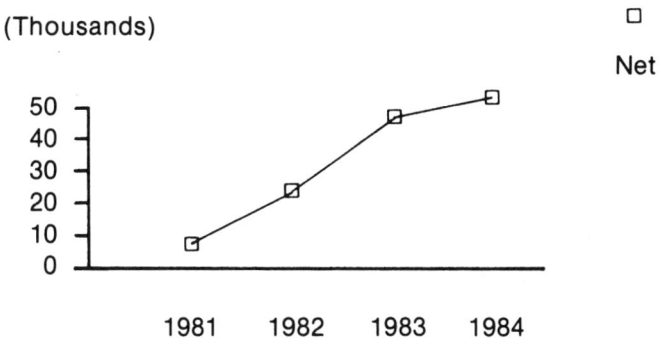

Figure 7.7.   Line graph

MARKED POINTS

A marked points graph resembles a line graph without the connecting line. Try graphing 1980 through 1984 net income as a marked points graph. Your graph should resemble that shown in figure 7.8.

X-Y

An X-Y graph is essentially a marked points graph based on the Cartesian coordinate system. As you may (or may not) recall from algebra, a value is plotted in the coordinate system using its X and Y values.

Before we begin experimenting with X-Y graphs, let's input the spreadsheet data shown in figure 7.9.

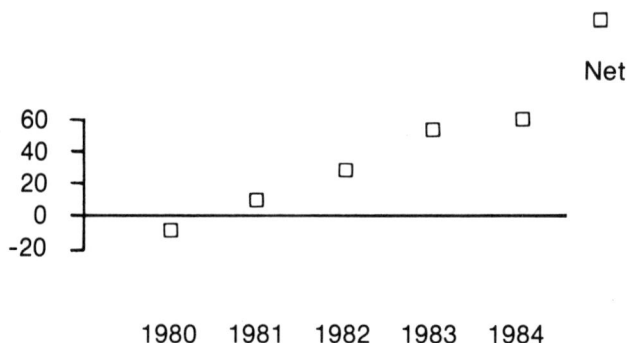

Figure 7.8. Marked points graph

	A	B	C	D
1	Gas % +or -	Prod. % +or- avg.		
2	-.85	-.25		
3	-.80	-.19		
4	-.45	-.13		
5	-.25	-.07		
6	-.09	-.01		
7	.15	.09		
8	.35	.26		
9	.65	.29		
10	.79	.31		

Figure 7.9. GAS spreadsheet

Column A indicates gas usage as a percentage above or below an average. Column B indicates productivity as a percentage above or below normal. Let's suppose an oil embargo broke out and your firm had to sharply curtail gas usage. You could display the probable effect of gas conservation on productivity pictorially using an X-Y graph as shown in figure 7.10.

An X-Y graph requires data from at least two or more adjacent columns or rows in a spreadsheet. Data must be specified as two or more adjacent columns in a data base. If more than two rows or columns are selected, each additional row or column is plotted against the first.

Notice that the X-Y graph's X and Y axes are numeric. The X-axis labels are derived from the first column or row selected for graphing.

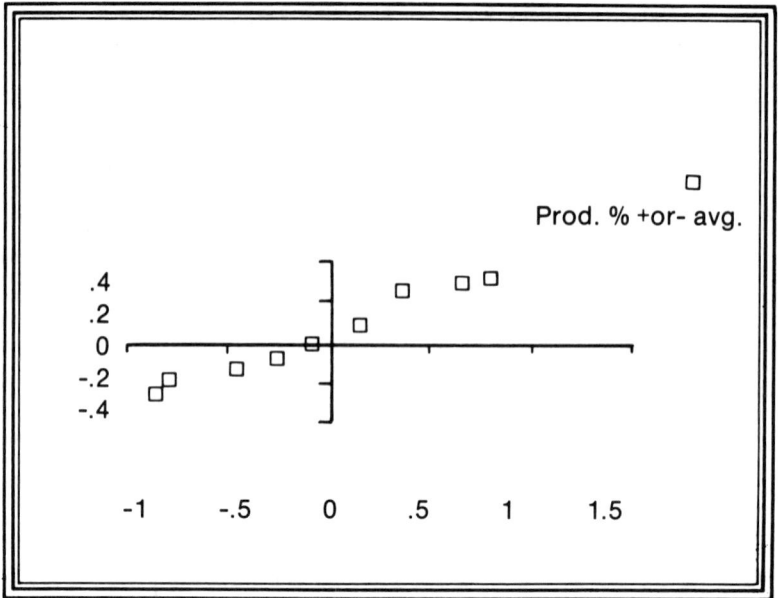

Figure 7.10. X-Y graph of effect of gas usage on productivity

Graphs Menu Options

In our discussion thus far, we've covered all of the Graphs menu selections except two:

> Add to Existing Graph
> Options

We will discuss "Add to Existing Graph" in the section entitled "Combining Graphs." We'll discuss the Options submenu in the following sections.

When Options is chosen from the Graphs menu by pressing [RET], the submenu shown in figure 7.11 is displayed.

X-axis Title	{ }
Y-axis Title	{ }
Manual Y-axis Scaling	
Lowest Y-axis Value	{ }
Highest X-axis Value	{ }
Scale in Increments of	{ }
Explode Pie Slice	{0}

Figure 7.11.   Graphs Options submenu

To exit this submenu, press the Right arrow key.

X-AXIS TITLE AND Y-AXIS TITLE

This option allows a title to be specified for either the X or Y-axis. Let's experiment by adding "Net Profits" as the Y-axis title for our NETINC graph.

1. Assuming GRAPHDAT is displayed on the desktop with the highlight in its border, press Ctrl-G O to display the Options submenu.
2. Use the cursor movement keys to position the highlight to Y-axis Title.* Press [RET] and enter Net Profits [RET]. Notice that Net Profits is displayed in the submenu.

* In some instances you may have to select Y-axis Title by pressing Y.

3. Press the Right arrow key to exit the submenu. Notice that you cannot select **Draw New Graph**. Press **ESC** to exit the Graphs menu. Proceed by selecting C3 through C7 from GRAPHDAT and drawing the graph with the Y-axis title. Your graph should appear as shown in figure 7.12.

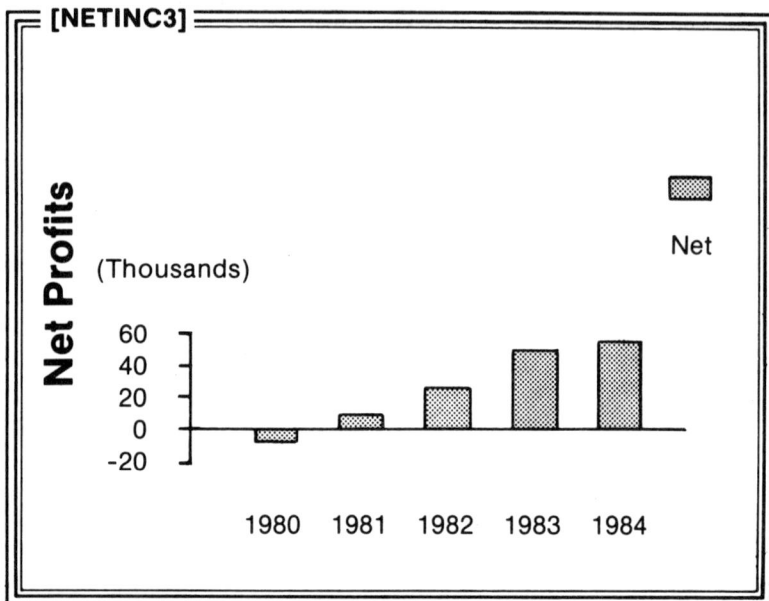

Figure 7.12. NETINC3 with Y-axis title

SCALING A GRAPH

Scaling refers to the numeric values used for the Y-axis. Framework generates the Y-axis scale automatically, but you have the option to set alternative scaling values using the Options submenu.

After choosing the Options submenu, enter values for:

Lowest Y-axis Value	-10,000
Highest Y-axis Value	70,000
Scale in Increments of	10,000

Notice the values entered are displayed in the Options submenu. Be sure the **Manual Y-axis Scaling** toggle is "ON" before you print the graph. Figure 7.13 depicts NETINC3 (as shown in 7.12) with a low Y-axis value of -10,000, a high Y-axis value of 70,000 and an increment of 10,000.

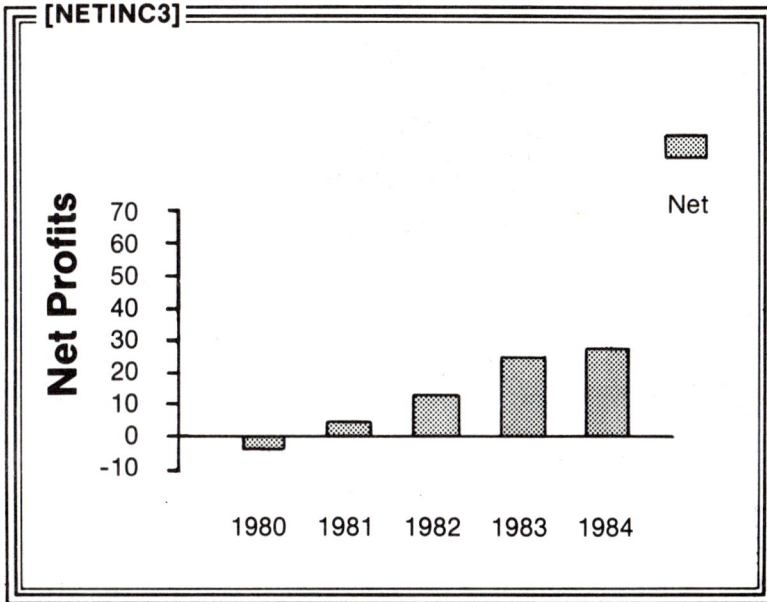

Figure 7.13.   NETINC3 with Y-axis scaling

EXPLODED PIE SLICE

The final Options submenu item enables you to specify one slice of a pie graph which is to be pulled away from the rest of the graph. The pie slices are numbered beginning at the "noon" position with 1 and continuing counterclockwise. Enter the number of the pie slice you want to pull out. An entry of -1 pulls out all of the slices; 0 results in none being pulled out.

[NETINC5]

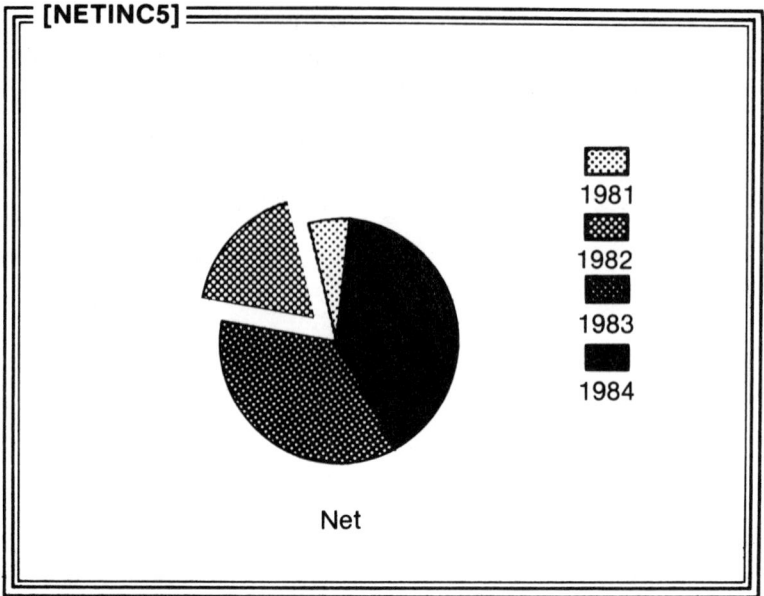

Figure 7.14. 1981 through 1984 net income with 1982 net income exploded

Figure 7.14 depicts 1981 through 1984 net income with 1982 net income exploded. A value of 2 was specified for **Explode Pie Slice**.

Combining Graphs

With Framework you can add one or more graphs onto an existing graph. These are known as graph overlays. When working with overlays, however, you must keep in mind that only line and marked points graphs can be used as overlays and the existing graph cannot be an X-Y or pie graph.

Let's use a new version of our NETINC graph to practice adding overlays. Remember that NETINC is a bar graph depicting 1980 through 1984 net income. Let's add a marked points graph overlay of gross income. Assuming that the GRAPHDAT spreadsheet is displayed on the desktop with the highlight on its border, observe the following steps:

1. Press [DOWNLEVEL] to move the highlight into the frame body. Position the highlight at C3. Press [F6-Extend Select] and extend the highlight through C7. Then press [RET].

2. Press Ins to open the Graphs menu. Be sure that Bar is toggled "ON". Select Draw New Graph and press [RET]. The following will be displayed in the message area:

   Press RETURN to draw a graph here, or
   select desired frame and press RETURN

   Press [RET] to draw the bar graph of 1980 through 1984 net income.

3. Move the highlight to the GRAPHDAT tray. The highlight will be flashing on the GRAPHDAT frame's border. Press [DOWNLEVEL] to enter the frame body. Cells C3 through C7 will be highlighted. Press the Left Arrow key to move the highlight to B3 through B7, gross income for 1980 through 1984. Press [F6-Extend Select] [RET] to select these cells.

4. Press INS to display the Graphs menu. Once Marked Points has been selected, select Add to Existing Graph and press [RET]. The following prompt will appear:

   Press RETURN to draw graph here, or
   select desired frame and press RETURN.

   Move the highlight to the untitled frame created in step 2 and press [RET]. The graph should appear as shown in figure 7.15. Let's title our graph NETINCOV.

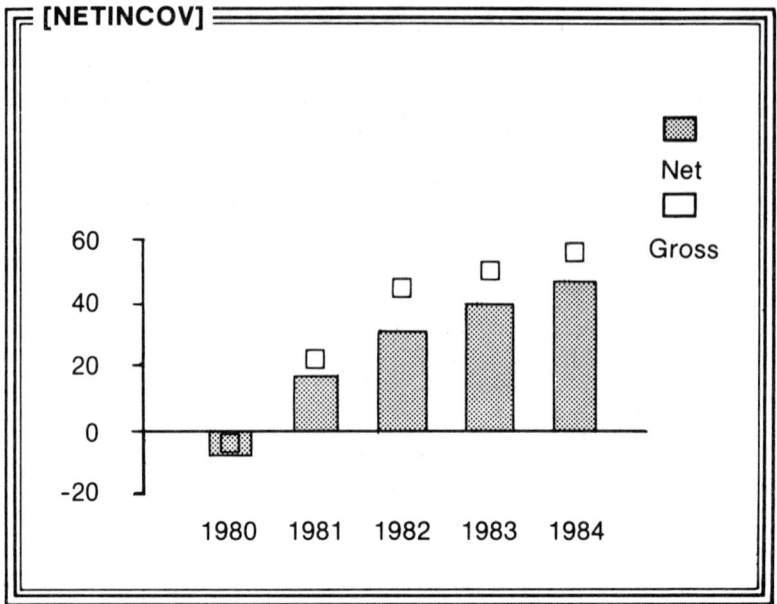

Figure 7.15. NETINCOV graph

@drawgraph

You've probably already noticed a formula beginning with @drawgraph in the status panel of the graph frames you've created. A graph is drawn as specified by the parameters contained in the @drawgraph function, which is created automatically when a graph is drawn using the Graphs menu. Each individual parameter is delimited with a comma.

You can change a graph by editing the @drawgraph formula in the message area. This eliminates the need to return to the spreadsheet or data base to select cells or fields and the Graphs menu to redraw the graph.

Assuming the current graph frame is NETINC, press [F2-Formula Edit] to display the @drawgraph function for editing. The following will appear in the message area:

@DRAWGRAPH(GRAPHDAT.C3:GRAPHDAT.C7,#COLUMN,#BAR,,,)

@drawgraph parameters are as follows for a Bar, Stacked Bar, Line, Marked Points, or X-Y graph:

@DRAWGRAPH (*area, rowcol, type, title, xtitle, ytitle, ylow, yhi, incr*)

The parameters for a pie graph are:

@DRAWGRAPH(*area, rowcol, type, title, xtitle, explode*)

area refers to the area of the spreadsheet or data base that is to be graphed. Notice that the spreadsheet or data base name is combined with the cell coordinate or field name respectively.

rowcol can either have a value of #ROW (X-axis labeled from row) or #COLUMN (X-axis labeled from column).

type refers to the graph type: #BAR, #STACKED BAR, #MARKED POINTS, #X-Y, or #PIE.

The remaining parameters are optional. *title* refers to a graph title. *xtitle* refers to an optional X-axis title. *ytitle* refers to an optional Y-axis title.

ylow refers to the low value for the Y-axis. *yhi* refers to the high value for the Y-axis. *incr* refers to the Y-axis incremental scale. *explode* references the number of the pie slice to explode. These are explained in the Graph Menu Options section.

Let's practice editing the @drawgraph formula. Suppose we wanted a pie chart of 1981 through 1984 net income. (Remember negative values aren't allowed in pie charts.) Observe the following steps to create this graph:

1. Press [F2-Edit Formula] to display the graph formula in the message area.

2. Press the Right arrow key until the cursor is positioned over the 3 in C3. Press 4 followed by [DEL].

3. Press the Right arrow key again until the cursor is positioned on the B in #BAR. Type PIE and press [DEL] three times.

4. Press [RET]. The graph will be redrawn as shown in figure 7.16.

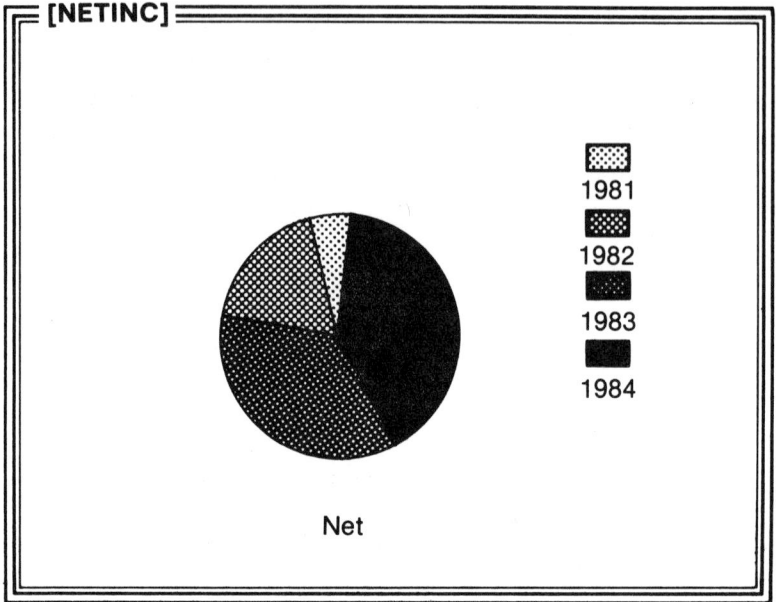

Figure 7.16. Pie chart of 1981-1984 net income

Using the [F2-Edit Formula] key, change the NETINC @drawgraph formula back to its original settings.

@DRAWGRAPH(GRAPHDAT.C3:GRAPHDAT.C7,#COLUMN,#BAR,,,)

Printing a Graph

A graph is printed in the same manner as text in Framework, by selecting Begin from the Print menu. The graph will be printed at the same size as it is displayed on the screen. You may wish to use [F4-Size] to adjust the graph's screen size so that the printed copy is the proper size.

Linking a Graph to Its Data Source

The @drawgraph function generally links the graph to its spreadsheet or data base source. You can have the graph frame automatically update itself when changes are made to its source data by entering the graph name in a spreadsheet cell. You can then update the graph by selecting its frame and pressing [F5-Recalc].

Let's illustrate this procedure with an example.

1. Assuming that **GRAPHDAT** is on the desktop with the highlight flashing in its border, press [DOWN-LEVEL] to move the highlight into the frame. Change cell **C7** to read **85,089**. Position the highlight at cell **D7**, and enter:

   @NETINC [RET]

   Notice that **#GRAPH** is displayed in **D7**. Following recalculation of this new formula, the NETINC graph is automatically redrawn.

2. Press [F5-Recalc] to redisplay the NETINC graph at any time.

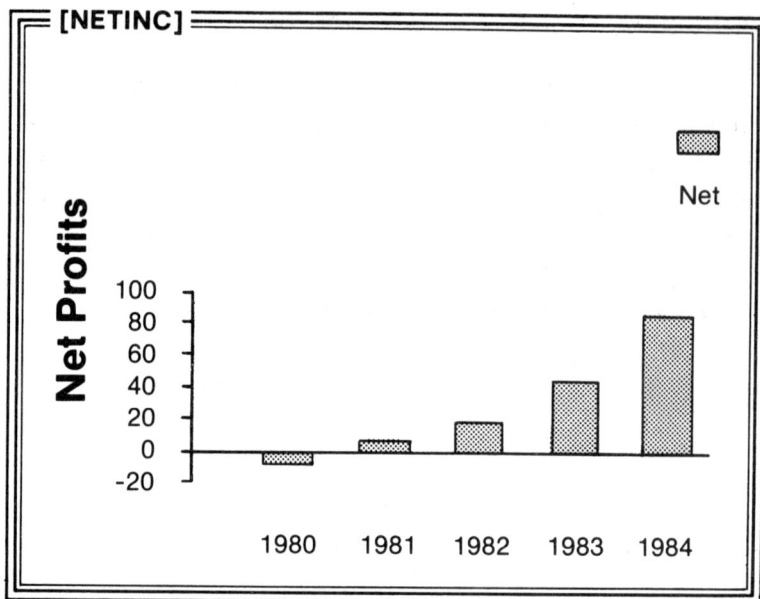

Figure 7.17. NETINC with revised 1984 net income

8

Communications

MITE/MS is a menu driven communications package included with Framework. Some of MITE's uses include:

- Accessing on-line timesharing systems and data bases
- Accessing on-line bulletin boards
- Exchanging files with remote computers

MITE can be used with most auto-dial/auto-answer modems as well as many manual dial modems.

MITE runs under MS-DOS or PC-DOS versions 2.0 and 2.1. Hardware requirements are 64K RAM and at least one floppy disk drive.

This chapter is divided into three major sections. The first deals with MITE usage via menus in the MS-DOS environment. The second section deals with MITE usage within the Framework environment. The final section deals with using local and remote commands to control a MITE session from a single terminal in the MS-DOS environment.

We found the easiest way to accomplish communications transfer was by using the remote and local commands to operate MITE in the terminal mode. In our opinion, using MITE in the menu mode or within the Framework environment is tedious and confusing due to the complexity of the menus. Therefore, we recommend use of the remote and local commands to effect MITE communications.

MITE TELECOMMUNICATIONS

MITE Usage

In the following sections, we intend to present step-by-step instructions on MITE usage. This discussion is designed as a concise alternative to the 100 plus pages which document MITE in the Framework manual.

This chapter neither discusses nor defines the terms and concepts that apply to communications. If you are a novice in the field of communications, you may wish to refer to chapters 1 and 2 in the MITE User's Guide before proceeding with this chapter.

The steps involved in a MITE remote file transfer are as follows:

1. The communications source must run MITE on his system. MITE must be set up so that data will be sent at the correct baud rate.

2. The source must dial the phone number of the destination terminal, the computer which is to receive the data being transferred. The destination computer must first be set up to receive the telephone communications.

3. The source specifies transmission protocol options. Afterwards, the file is transmitted to the destination terminal.

4. When the file has been received by the destination terminal, the source hangs up.

Before explaining these steps in more detail, we will explain the process of copying the MITE master disk.

COPYING THE MITE MASTER DISK

You should avoid using your MITE master diskette during a communications session as it could be damaged accidentally. Observe the following steps to create a working copy of MITE:

1. Place your DOS system disk in drive A and a blank disk in drive B.

2. Use the following command to format the blank disk so that it contains the DOS system files:

FORMAT B:/S

3. Remove the DOS system disk from A and replace it with the newly formatted disk from B, which should now be bootable. Place Framework's System Disk #2* in drive B.

4. Press [Ctrl]-[Alt]-[Del] to reboot DOS.

---

* In the Framework manual, the user is instructed to place the MITE Master disk in drive B. The MITE files in this author's Framework system were resident on System Disk #2.

5. Type the following command to transfer MITE.EXE to the diskette in drive A:

    COPY B:MITE.EXE A:

6. Type the following command to transfer MITE-NULL.HLP to the diskette in drive A:

    COPY B:MITENULL.HLP A:

7. Type the following command:

    COPY B:*.PAR A:

    to copy the following files to A:

    MITE.PAR
    ANSWER.PAR
    COMPUSRV.PAR
    DOWJONES.PAR
    JOESPC.PAR
    SOURCE.PAR
    TELEMAIL.PAR

8. Remove System Disk #2 from drive B and return it to its protective envelope.

If you examine the directory of your MITE working diskette in drive A, you'll find that it contains the following files:

```
COMMAND   COM   17792   10-20-83   12:00p
MITE      EXE   35840    6-27-84   11:41a
MITE      PAR     896    6-05-84    2:20p
MITENULL  HLP     616    6-28-84    9:08p
ANSWER    PAR     896    7-11-84    2:18p
COMPUSRV  PAR     896    5-31-84   10:16a
DOWJONES  PAR     896    5-31-84   10:15a
JOESPC    PAR     896    5-31-84   10:12a
SOURCE    PAR     896    5-31-84   10:14a
TELEMAIL  PAR     896    5-31-84   10:13a
```

INSTALLING MITE

In this section, we'll describe the installation procedure for MITE when the program is to be used for modem communications to another computer equipped with MITE. This installation procedure can be successfully used with most auto-dial/auto-answer modems. If this installation procedure does not work for your particular modem, refer to the **MITE User's Guide**, Mycroft Labs or your dealer for additional information and/or assistance. Also note that in certain instances, it may be necessary for you to reset the modem's dip switches in order for it to be used successfully with MITE.

1. Insert the MITE working disk in drive A and reboot the system by pressing [Ctrl]-[Alt] and [Del].
2. When the A> prompt reappears, enter MITE [RET]. Mite's main menu will appear as shown in figure 8.1 (assuming that a modem is connected to the system).

Let's examine the menu's first three lines. The first line, of course, contains copyright, title, and version information. The left-hand side of the second line should contain the word OFFLINE, which indicates that the computer does not sense a connection with another computer.

It's possible that the word ONLINE will appear rather than OFFLINE. This is often the result of using a manual dial modem or using improper cabling or switch settings with your auto-dial modem.

To alleviate this problem, there are generally two troubleshooting procedures.

The first step is to confirm that the Comm port setting in the Mite Special Features Menu agrees with the com port being used by your hardware. There are two com ports available in MS-DOS, com 1 and com 2. Press T to display the Special Features Menu and confirm that the number displayed for option C — Comm Port agrees with the com number of your hardware communication port.

```
MITE v2.80  -  Copyright (c) 1983, Mycroft Labs, Inc.
ONLINE . Bytes Captured =      0/65520. Capture = OFF.
Site ID =

MAIN MENU

        G - Go Start Communications
        H - Hangup Phone
        I - Enter Site ID
        L - Load Parameters from Disk File
        S - Save Parameters on Disk File

                Sub-Menus:

        P - Parameter        O - Option
        U - Text File Upload  D - Text File Download
        B - Binary File Xfer  M - Macro Definition
        C - Command Processor F - Character Filter
        T - Special Features

        X - Exit to Operating System

Enter option (? for help):
```

Figure 8.1. Mite main menu

The next step is to check the configuration switches of the modem. Many of the "smart" modems available today have a configuration switch which controls the **carrier detect** lead. The **carrier detect** lead notifies the computer when a carrier signal has been received back from the device to which a connection is being attempted. When this signal is detected, the computer becomes "on-line" and can transmit or receive data. Many of today's "smart" modems fool the computer by telling it the **carrier detect** lead is on at all times. This allows the "smart" modems to transmit and receive their own special control characters prior to an actual connection between the computers.

Of course this also fools MITE and the ONLINE status appears at all times on the second line of the screen display. By resetting the configuration switch which controls the **carrier**

detect lead, most "smart" modems will operate in a normal mode. For example, a Hayes Smartmodem™ can be switched to the offline mode by setting switch 6 in the up position.

    3. Select P for Parameter menu. The menu depicted in figure 8.2 will appear. The Parameter menu contains information required by Mite to transfer data.

    4. Your first Parameter menu entry is the baud rate. Note that the baud rate is set at 1200, which is standard for most personal computer data communications. If we wanted to change the baud rate, we could do so by pressing B followed by the desired rate.

    Type a new baud rate, 300, and press [RET].

If your modem is manual dial, you can skip steps 5 through 7. These steps are only applicable for auto-dial modems.

```
MITE v2.80  --  Copyright (c) 1983, Mycroft Labs, Inc.
OFFLINE. Bytes Captured =      0/65520. Capture = OFF.
Site ID =

PARAMETER MENU

        B - Baud Rate              =  1200
        D - Data Bits              = 7
        P - Parity                 = EVEN
        S - Stop Bits              = 1

        R - Role (ANS/ORG)         = ORG
        E - Entry Password         =
        M - Mode (Duplex)          = FULL

        A - Auto Redial Count      = 0
        N - Phone Number           =
        I - Modem Init String      =
        H - Dial Prefix            = AT DT

        X - Exit to main menu

Enter option (? for help):
```

Figure 8.2. Parameter menu

5. Your next step is to enter the Modem Init String (I in the Parameter menu) if required. The Modem Init Strings for a number of widely used modems are listed in table 8.1.

Table 8.1. Modem Init String Dial Prefix values

Modem	Modem Init String*	Dial Prefix*
Anchor Signalman Mark VII	None	None
BIZCOMP 1012	None	None
CTS 212AH	None	Q MD
Datec 212	None	AT
Hayes Smartmodem	None	AT D
Incomm 212A	None	AT D
Novation Smart-Cat	%I	"%D" *
Novation Auto- or J-Cat	None	None
Rixon 212A	M MNU	AT D
Toyocom (BYTCOMM) 212AD	M MQ	Q M MD
UDS 212A/D	OG0	OG0END
U.S. Robotics 212	None	AT D

6. The next step is to enter the dial prefix (H in the Parameter menu). The dial prefixes are also listed in table 8.1. Press H and note the following prompt:

Enter dial header string:

Enter the dial prefix for your modem.

7. The next step is to enter the phone number you wish to communicate with. Choose the N option and type in the number followed by [RET].

Refer to your modem's manual to verify that the phone number was entered using the proper syntax.

* In MITE, alphabetic characters must be entered in upper case.

We're now ready to exit the Parameter menu. Before doing so, note the R-Role(ANS/ORG) entry in the Parameter menu. If your computer will be calling another computer, this choice should be set to ORG. If your computer will be receiving data from another computer, the setting should be ANS.

8. Press X to exit to the main menu.

9. Before proceeding we need to change one parameter in the Binary File Xfer menu. Type B to access the menu. Notice the protocol is set to XMODEM. XMODEM is generally used on CP/M machines. Since we're accessing an MS-DOS computer equipped with MITE, another choice is in order. Press P to display the following entry options:

X — XMODEM (Single)   B — XMODEM/B (Batch)
C — CLINK & Crosstalk   H — HAYES (Smartcom)
I — IBMPC Async   M — MITE Multi-file
T — TEXT (mainframe)

These are explained in chapter 8 of your MITE User's Guide. We'll choose M for our example.

10. Press X to exit to the main menu.

11. We've now completed the parameter entry process. At this point, we should save our parameter settings for future use. Enter S. When prompted for the filename, type in:

Mite1 [RET]

You can alter this file at any time by merely loading it using the L parameter.

Making The Connection

We're now ready to actually send our file. Once your modem has been properly cabled, and the message OFF LINE appears on the second line of the screen, observe the following steps:

184 Framework User's Handbook

1. After accessing the main menu, press G. MITE will dial the remote computer and attempt to connect to its modem. Of course the remote device must be prepared to receive a transmission.

2. The following message will then appear on your screen:

Carrier Detected

when the remote device returns a carrier signal.

3. Return to the main menu by pressing [CTRL]-J. Doing so will not disconnect you from the remote computer. Choose U-Text File Upload to display the Text File Upload menu.

4. When this menu appears, again type U-Upload Text File. You will be prompted for the filename. Enter the filename with drive specifier B if necessary and press [RET]. MITE will send the file to the receiving computer.

6. When the transmission is completed the following message is displayed:

Transmission Complete

7. Press [CTRL]-J to return to the main menu.

ANSWERING A REMOTE TERMINAL

To change the Mite function from connecting to another terminal to receiving a connection, only one parameter must be changed.

1. Enter P to access the parameter menu.

2. Reset the baud rate or any of the other communication parameteres to match the dialing terminal.

3. Enter R-Role to change this option from ORGinator to ANSwer.

4. Press X to exit to the main menu.

5. To enter the answer mode, press G — Go Start Communications.

The terminal will now respond to any attempts to connect to its phone number.

CAPTURING DATA

Once a connection is made, all transmissions, from either the keyboard or disk files, will appear on each computer's screen. To capture the transmission on disk file, the receiving computer must be set to the capture mode.

1. Press [CTRL]-J to return to the main menu without terminating the connection.
2. Press D — Text File Download.
3. Press C — Capture Mode to turn the capture mode on and display the following prompt:
   Enter Filename:
4. Type in a name for the disk file and press [RET].
5. Press X to return to the main menu.
6. Press G to resume the transmission.

Any keyboard entries or disk files transmitted from the remote computer will be saved on the disk file named in the Capture command.

MITE KEYBOARD CONVENTIONS

The function keys have a different meaning in MITE than in Framework. When you use MITE to establish a communications connection, the function key assignments listed in table 8.2 will be active.

The function key assignments described in table 8.2 are set in parameter files supplied on Framework's System Disk #2.

Table 8.2. MITE Function Key Assignments

Function Key	Description
F1	Displays a directory of prepared frames
F2	Signs off, disconnects and returns to Framework
F3	Starts Text Send operation
F4	Starts Text Capture operation
F5	Ends Text Capture
F6-F8	Reserved
F9	Accesses MITE main menu
F10	Logon sequence

You can redefine these key assignments by using MITE's macro definition menu as described in chapter 9 of the **MITE User's Guide**. Remember that the 10 available macro settings are numbered 0 through 9 while the 10 available function keys are numbered 1 through 10. Therefore F1 would correspond to macro #0; F2 to macro #1, etc.

Several other keyboard entries are useful during a MITE session. [CTRL]-J can be used (like F9) to access MITE's main menu. [CTRL]-B sends a break signal [CTRL]-K initiates a local command. [CTRL]-R initiates a remote command.

In certain instances you might wish to send one of these codes to the computer you are communicating with. You can nullify a control code's special meaning in MITE by pressing ESC prior to control code entry.

CONCLUSION

MITE offers numerous options of which we've only discussed a few. Refer to the MITE User's Guide for more information about MITE's various options and the ways in which the package can be used.

FRAMEWORK TELECOMMUNICATIONS

Now that we've examined how MITE functions under DOS, let's explore how it works in the Framework environment.

Installing MITE in Framework

Your first step in using MITE in the Framework environment is to install it. Follow the procedure described in "Installing Telecommunications" in chapter 1.

Once MITE has been properly installed, a file named UTIL.FW will reside on your Framework System Disk #2. When you subsequently load Framework, UTIL will automatically be displayed in its tray on the desktop after start-up.

Telecommunications Submenu

Once MITE has been installed, the Telecommunications Submenu will be available in the Disk menu. With the highlight on Utilities in the Disk menu, press [RET] to display the submenu as shown in figure 8.3.

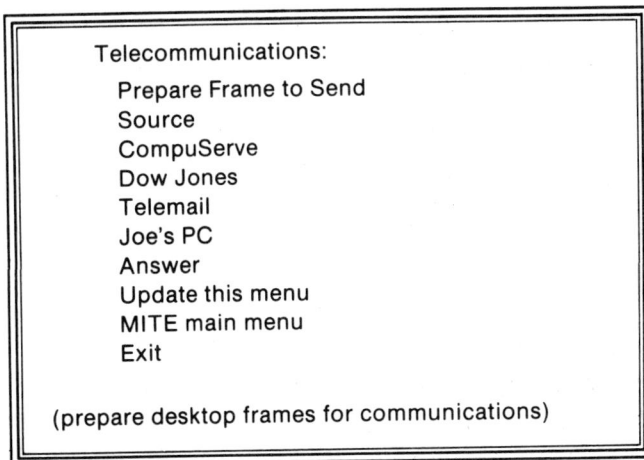

```
Telecommunications:
    Prepare Frame to Send
    Source
    CompuServe
    Dow Jones
    Telemail
    Joe's PC
    Answer
    Update this menu
    MITE main menu
    Exit

(prepare desktop frames for communications)
```

Figure 8.3.   Telecommunications submenu

We will discuss the submenu options in the following sections.

PREPARE FRAME TO SEND

If you intend to send one or more desktop frames to another computer, you must select the frames before establishing a communications link. The frames to be selected must have been loaded into the desktop prior to choosing Telecommunications from the Disk menu.

Your first step in selecting a frame for telecommunications is to select "Prepare Frame to Send" from the Telecommunications submenu. The desktop is then displayed with the following message;

Enter frame name to prepare (or CURSOR POINT ↑); RETURN finishes

Next enter the name of the frame you want selected for communications. Let's assume we want to select TRY1.FW (from chapter 4) which is located on a data disk in drive B. Enter TRY1 and press [RET]. The following message will then appear:

Text format Binary format
(prepare for interactive systems, electronic mail, etc)

In Framework you have the option of sending a file either in text or binary format. For our purposes let's specify text. Framework will write TRY1 with the extension .F$T to the diskette in drive B. Binary files are written with the extension .F$B.

After TRY1.F$T has been written to disk, the Telecommunications submenu will again be displayed. You can again choose Prepare Frame to Send to select another frame for communications, or you can send the selected frame (TRY1.F$T) to a remote computer.

SOURCE, COMPUSERVE, DOW JONES, TELEMAIL

These options enable you to exit the Framework environment to MITE telecommunications and connect with a communications service without losing the contents of the desktop. The desktop is saved as DESKTOP.FW. When MITE is exited, the original desktop is restored from DESKTOP.FW.

The MITE parameter files associated with these menu items must be altered to include items such as your ID number, local access code, etc.

JOE'S PC

This submenu option allows you to establish a communications connection with another computer. Again the desktop is saved as DESKTOP.FW prior to accessing MITE. The MITE program goes directly into terminal mode and automatically dials the phone number specified in the Mite Parameter file. In order to dial the remote system, a parameter file must first be created for each computer to be accessed and the Telecommunications submenu must have been updated as described in "Update This Menu" on the following page.

ANSWER

Choosing "Answer" from the Telecommunications submenu places your computer in the answer terminal mode. The desktop is saved prior to exiting Framework to MITE.

A MITE Framework system can be accessed by another computer while it is unattended. The system initiating the connection can transfer files to or from the remote system without any operator intervention on the remote system. Refer to chapter 14 of your MITE User's Guide for more information on setting up an unattended answer system.

UPDATE THIS MENU

This submenu selection allows you to add or delete items in the Telecommunications submenu. When Update is selected, the menu items that can be added or deleted are displayed on the desktop. The following characters appear in the message area:

↑ ↓ Add Delete Exit and Save

Use the right and left arrow keys to move the highlight in the message area. The up and down arrow keys move the highlight up and down in the list of submenu selections.

Notice that as you move this highlight, the associated parameter filename is displayed on the Status line. When you add a Telecommunication submenu item, you are, in effect, creating a connection between Framework and a MITE parameter file.

If you choose Add from the message area, a new menu item will be created immediately below the highlight. You will be prompted for the submenu item's name and the MITE parameter filename. The submenu item will be created after you have responded to these prompts.

To delete a submenu selection, highlight it and select Delete. You will be asked to verify the deletion. Upon verification the selection will be deleted.

To return to the Telecommunications submenu, choose Exit and Save and press [RET]. The submenu changes will be saved and the Telecommunications submenu will again be displayed.

MITE MAIN MENU

This submenu item allows you to access the MITE main menu. Since the desktop is saved prior to exiting Framework, when you exit MITE the current desktop display will reappear.

CUSTOMIZING TELECOMMUNICATIONS SUBMENU ITEMS

As we mentioned earlier, MITE includes a number of parameter files that are already configured for a communications service. These include:

```
COMPUSRV.PAR
DOWJONES.PAR
SOURCE.PAR
TELEMAIL.PAR
```

You can determine the PAR files by using the following DOS command:

```
DIR *.PAR
```

or by choosing **Update This File** from the Telecommunications submenu.

Since the parameter files have been preconfigured for use with a Hayes Smartmodem 1200 at 1200 baud and since most services require that you input your local access number, you will almost always have to reconfigure these for use with your system. Fortunately, reconfiguring the parameter files is a simple process. Let's illustrate by reconfiguring SOURCE. PAR. Assuming that you were in the Telecommunications Submenu, observe the following steps:

1. Choose **Update This Menu** from the Telecommunications submenu. Notice that the submenu items associated with parameter files are displayed on the desktop. Move the highlight to **Source**. Notice the parameter filename SOURCE.PAR which is included in the @UTIL function in the status panel.

2. Choose **Exit and Save** to return to the Telecommunications submenu. Select the **MITE main menu**. After the desktop is saved, the MITE main menu will appear.

3. Choose L from the MITE main menu. The following prompt will appear:

Enter Filename:

Key in SOURCE.PAR. After the file has been loaded, choose P from the MITE main menu to display the present parameter file information shown in figure 8.4.

Notice that you must enter your local access number. You may also wish to change the baud rate and dial prefix depending on the type of modem you are using.

4. When the desired changes have been made, return to the MITE main menu and press S. The following prompt will appear:

Enter filename:

Save the revised parameter file as SOURCE.PAR.

```
MITE v2.80  -  Copyright (c) 1983, Mycroft Labs, Inc.
ONLINE . Bytes Captured =     0/ 9696. Capture = OFF.
Site ID = The Source via TELENET

PARAMETER MENU

        B - Baud Rate           =  1200
        D - Data Bits           = 7
        P - Parity              = EVEN
        S - Stop Bits           = 1

        R - Role (ANS/ORG)       = ORG
        E - Entry Password       =
        M - Mode (Duplex)        = FULL

        A - Auto Redial Count = 0
        N - Phone Number         = Enter Local Telenet Access Num
        I - Modem Init String =
        H - Dial Prefix          = AT DT

        X - Exit to main menu

Enter option (? for help):
```

Figure 8.4. SOURCE.PAR parameter menu

USING LOCAL AND REMOTE COMMANDS TO OPERATE MITE IN THE TERMINAL MODE

In our opinion the easiest method of accomplishing communications within Framework is to access MITE in the terminal mode and effect the communications transfer using local and remote commands. Local and remote commands provide MITE with the same information as menu entries. The advantage to local and remote commands is that the information is provided in an easier, more direct manner.

Local and remote commands can only be entered when MITE is in the terminal mode. Terminal mode can be defined as a situation where one computer, with MITE executing, acts as a terminal to a remote computer. In other words, characters entered on one computer are sent to the remote computer without these being interpreted by the originating system.

Certain keystrokes are, however, interpreted by the originating system in the terminal mode. For instance if [CAPS LOCK] is on, lower case letters will still be generated as upper case. Also, **trigger** characters (see chapter 5 in the MITE User's Guide) will be interpreted by the originating system and will not be communicated to the remote system.

To enter the terminal mode, access MITE's main menu on the originating system and press G (for Go). If the remote system is running MITE, that system must also enter the terminal mode by entering G from the main menu. If the remote system is not running MITE, an action may or may not be needed on that system to establish a communications link depending on the communications software being used.

Entering a Local Command

To enter a local command in the terminal mode, the local command trigger character must first be entered. The default trigger character is ^ K, although this can be changed via the

Options menu. When the local command trigger character is entered on the local terminal, the following prompt is displayed:

Local Command?

The user may then enter the desired local command (see page 195). Note that only the first four characters of the local command need be entered. If a filename is required, MITE will automatically prompt for it later. Once the local command has been executed, the terminal mode will again take effect.

Entering a Remote Command

Remote commands allow the local system to access the remote system and control its actions through standard Mite commands. This allows the remote system to be left unattended. When the call is answered by the remote terminal, the remote trigger character is displayed in the MITE header on the originating system.

The default remote trigger character is ^R. This can be changed in the option menu. Upon entry of the remote trigger character on either the local or remote system, the following prompt is displayed:

Remote Command?

At this point either user can enter a command which subsequently will be executed by the other system. Output from the command is displayed by both systems.

The remote commands are identical to the local commands with one exception. Exit cannot be used as a remote command.

Remote and Local Commands

APPEnd

This command enables the user to write transferred data to a disk file without closing that file. The Capture mode must be on prior to issuing APPEnd and is left on after the data has been written. The disk file is not closed by APPEnd. Therefore, a subsequent APPEnd or WRITe can be undertaken for that file. APPEnd is the equivalent of the Text File Download Menu's A option.

BUFFer

Displays information on the printer buffer.

CAPTure ON or CAPTure OFF

These commands can be used to turn the text capture mode on or off. A filename will be prompted for when CAPTure ON is first specified or after an initial WRITe. These remote commands are the equivalent of the Text File Download Menu's C option.

CRC ON or CRC OFF

These commands allow the user to turn on or turn off CRC error checking for either of the two XMODEM protocols. These are the equivalent of the Binary File Transfer Menu's C option.

ECHO ON or ECHO OFF

This command controls the printer echo feature. When echo is on, the transmitted data is sent to the printer device as well as the screen. This command corresponds to option P on the Text File Download Menu.

196 Framework User's Handbook

EXIT

Returns from Mite to the computer's operating system. Any open files are automatically closed.

HELP or HELP S

Displays the local and system commands, respectively.

MACRos

Displays the non-blank macro strings.

PROTocol

Displays the existing binary protocol along with a listing of the available protocols. A new protocol is selected by entering the letter which corresponds to the desired protocol. This is equivalent to the P option on the Binary File Transfer Menu.

READ

Sends a specified file from disk as if it were entered from the local terminal keyboard. An optional disk drive name may be specified before the filename followed by a colon if the desired file is not contained in the current drive. Read is the equivalent of the Text File Upload Menu option U.

RECV

Reads a transmitted file to a disk file. Mite binary transfer protocol will ignore the user specified filename and use the filename specified on the Sending System. The Binary Transfer Menu option R is its equivalent.

SCREen OFF or SCREen ON

The SCREen command controls the screen echo. When turned off, characters transmitted from the sending system will not appear on the screen.

SEND

Transmits a specified file from disk to the remote terminal. If the file is not in the current drive, specify the drive followed by a colon and then the filename. SEND is equivalent to the S option of the Binary File Transfer Menu.

USE

Transfer input control from the keyboard to a input file. Input will be obtained from the file, instead of the keyboard, until the end of the file is encountered.

WRITE

WRITe closes a disk file opened with the APPEnd command and turns the capture mode off. The Text File Download Menu option W is its equivalent.

Initiating a Local/Remote Communication Session

We used two IBM PC computers equipped with the Hayes Smartmodem for the Mite Local/Remote Communication Session. You may have to use a different protocol to suit your modem type.

1 2 3 4 5 6 7 8

Configuration
Switches

Up
Down

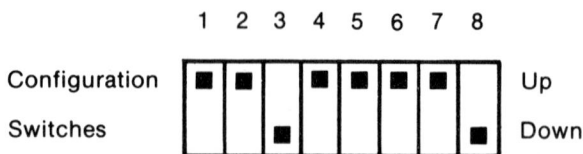

Figure 8.5. Hayes Smartmodem Switch Settings

To connect the Local and Remote terminals, follow the steps below for the remote terminal first and then for the local terminal.

1. With the Mite program disk in drive A, type in:

    A> Mite [RET]

2. Enter [P] to access the Parameter Menu

3. Set the appropriate communication parameters:

    Remote Terminal:

    1. Enter [B] — Baud Rate and type in 300 [RET].

    2. Enter [R] — Role which changes to ANSwer mode.

    3. Enter [X] to return to the main menu

    Local Terminal:

    1. Enter [B] — Baud Rate and type in 300 [RET].

    2. Enter [N] — Phone Number of the remote terminal

    3. Enter [X] to return to the main menu

4. Attempt to connect the devices by pressing [G] — Go
   Start Communications

When a successful connection occurs, the message "CONNECTED" appears on each terminal.

Controlling the Session

Generally, commands are issued to the remote system first so that it is prepared to react to the actions of the local system.

We will illustrate the process of controlling both the remote and local systems from one terminal using a simple file transfer. In chapter 4 a word processing frame, TRY1.FW, was created. Let's send a copy of that disk file to the remote system.

1. Enter ^R and the prompt:

   Remote Command?

   is displayed on the screen.

2. Type in PROT [RET] to display the current protocol and the available options.

3. Enter H — Hayes (Smartmodem) to select the Hayes Smartmodem protocol.

4. Repeat Steps 1 through 3 substituting ^K for ^R. Notice the prompt:

   Local Command?

   is displayed on the screen.

5. Enter ^R and type in RECV [RET]. The prompt:

   Enter filename:

   will be displayed.

6. Type in TRY1.FW [RET] or any other filename you wish to use. If you want to write the file to a disk other than the Mite program disk, remove the Mite disk and replace it with the desired disk.

7. Enter ^K and type in SEND [RET]. The prompt:

   Enter Filename:

   will appear.

8. Type in TRY1.FW [RET] with the disk containing that file in the currently selected disk drive.

Dots will slowly appear across the line below the filename prompt. Depending on the file size, these dots may extend down to the next line. When the transfer is complete, these messages appear:

Local	Remote
Local	**Remote**
File Sent	File Received
Resuming Link	Resuming Link

9. Enter ^ K and type in EXIT [RET] to end the communication session.

9
FRED Programming Language

The FRED programming language adds another dimension to the usage of integrated application software. While the Macro function has enabled spreadsheet users to perform programming within various integrated packages, the task was often awkward and time consuming in comparison to programming languages. All of the amenities which allow efficient and effective programming from various refined programming languages were simply not available in the integrated software environments.

With the introduction of Framework by ASHTON-TATE, a new programming language for integrated application software has been introduced. FRED combines the power and refinements of a programming language such as BASIC or FORTRAN with the integrated environment of Framework.

Components of a FRED Program

All of the Framework commands which were previously introduced are available in the FRED language. The FRED language is merely an extension of the Framework command language and can be used immediately by anyone experienced with Framework commands.

Just as any Framework application, a FRED program is based on frames. The program itself is entered, using the F2-Edit/Formula key, as a formula. Since any type of frame will accept formulas, FRED programs can be entered in spreadsheet, data base, or word frames. The rules or syntax for entering the FRED programs are generally the same as those which apply to the normal use of these frames.

A typical FRED program consists of three basic components: frame values, references and operators.

Frame Values

As we have learned in previous chapters, frames can contain either numeric or text values. Text values, often referred to as a "string," are enclosed in quote marks (" ") to differentiate them from numeric values.

In addition to numeric and text values, the FRED language defines another value type, a constant. The FRED constants are generally used to indicate the results from the evaluation of a formula. They can also be used to input values for the evaluation of formulas.

Type	Name	Definition
Formula	#FUNCTION	Results from calling a function which contains either @item or @return function calls
	#GRAPH	Contains values from a recalculated graph
	#KEY	Results when a key value is returned as the product of an @nextkey or @setmacro function
	#FILTER	Results when @filter is the last function executed in the recalculation of a formula
	#PICTURE	Same as #GRAPH
Graphing	#ROW/#COLUMN	Specifies X-axis labels from row or column labels
	#BAR/#LINE/ #MARKEDBAR/ #XY/#PIE	Specifies graph type
Macro	#ON/#OFF	Used by the @echo function to set screen echo
Logical	#YES/#NO #TRUE/#FALSE	Results from expressions involving relational operators such as equals (=) or less than (<)/greater than (>)
Postional	#BEFORE/#AFTER	Used by the @unit function to position a currency symbol before or after numbers displayed as Currency

Continued on next page

Figure 9.1. FRED Constants

Type	Name	Definition
Error	#DIV/0!	Expression contains an illegal operation which causes a division by zero
	#N/A!	Signifies a value is unavailable. Can occur when no value exists in the referenced frame or when a formula contains an error.
	#NAME?	Results from a reference to a frame not contained on the desktop
	#NULL!	Appears when the end of a regional reference is reached. Similar to end-of-file in other program languages. Also appears when a parameter is referenced in a FRED program but is not passed from the calling program
	#NUM!	Results from the illegal use of a numeric function
	#REF!	Occurs when a referenced frame cannot be found
	#TBD!	User definable error constant

Figure 9.1. (cont.) FRED Constants

All FRED constants begin with the number sign, #. They can be grouped into six catagories: formula, graphing, macro, logical, position and error. The formula constants are generally used to store the results of a formula evaluation. For example, #GRAPH and #PICTURE store the values of a recalculated graph. The various formula constants are stored in the frame where the formula has been recalculated.

The graphing constants are used by the @drawgraph function as parameters to define the graphing choices. For example, #STACKBAR will select the graph type, stacked bar.

The two macro constants, #ON and #OFF, control the @echo function. These constants determine whether the results of keystrokes are displayed on the screen.

The logical constants are simply #YES and #NO or #TRUE and #FALSE. They normally result from formulas involving relational operators such as equals (=) or less than ($<$) / greater than ($>$).

The positional constants, #BEFORE and #AFTER, are used by the @unit function to position a currency symbol or other legend before or after numbers displayed as Currency.

The error constants help the Framework user identify and correct errors in their FRED programs. The error constants will display for certain errors that commonly occur in FRED programs.

References

Referencing of coordinates and regions of coordinates is the most common method of building spreadsheet formulas. It is also an integral part of programming in the FRED language.

One situation where referencing with FRED can be utilized is when data from a separate frame must be located in order to complete the formulas in the current frame. For example, you might set up one frame called "ASSUMP-TIONS" which contains a program's constants for interest rates, inflation rate, internal rate of return, etc.

If you subsequently wanted to use one of the ASSUMP-TIONS values in another frame, you could do so by referencing the ASSUMPTIONS frame. Of course you could simply reenter the desired value in the new frame. However if the ASSUMPTIONS value was subsequently changed, the value in the new frame would not be automatically updated. You would have to enter the new value.

On the other hand, by referencing the ASSUMPTIONS frame, the value will automatically change if the ASSUMP-TONS frame is changed. In other words the FRED program will **look up** the revised value. Obviously referencing is the preferred method of specifying constant values.

REFERENCE LOOK UP RULES

Since Framework applications can consist of many frames, there are several rules which control the manner in which a search is conducted. The frame reference can consist of one or more frame names joined by periods (.). Each frame name specifies a step down the hierarchy to the desired frame, which is listed at the end. Framework begins its search from the frame where the formula is being evaluated. This is often referred to as the ANCHOR.

The first step is to search from the parent of the ANCHOR frame which is being evaluated. If no successful find occurs, then the next level parent is searched. The search continues up the hierarchy until a match is found or the desktop is reached.

COORDINATE AND REGION REFERENCES

Once the proper frame is reached, the reference may also specify a specific cell coordinate or region. For example, to search the REPORTS frame for COMMISSIONS during the month of MAY paid to a Mr. Jones, the following reference would be made:

REPORTS.COMMISSIONS.MAY.B4

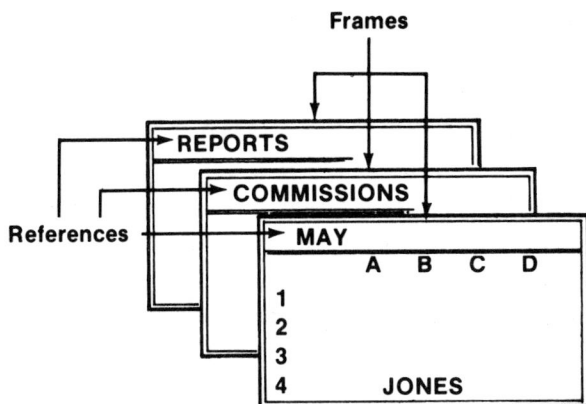

Figure 9.2. Coordinate Reference

To obtain an average commission for the month of May, a region of cells could be referenced.

@avg(REPORTS.COMMISSIONS.MAY.A1:D4)

The Region Operator (:) must be used when referencing a range of cells. The reference to average May commissions includes all cells between A1 and D4. The @average function computes the average commission for this group of cells.

Operators

Operators are used in the FRED language to identify the operations to perform with values and references. Figure 9.3 lists the various operators in four groups; arithmetic, string, relational, and special; by their order of precedence.

The arithmetic operators return a new value by taking the values or references on either side of the operator and performing the mathematical operation as indicated. The plus and minus operators may also be used with numeric data to indicate sign, positive or negative.

The ampersand (&) is used to combine two or more text strings. It serves to combine the values or references on either side into one continuous string.

Relational operators are used to compare numeric data to other numeric data or string data to other string data. When numeric and string data are compared, the relationship will always yield #FALSE. The operators compare the values or references on either side and return a #TRUE or #FALSE response based on their relationship.

String comparisons follow this set of rules:

- Capitalization is ignored (a is equivalent to A)
- The earlier the letter in the alphabet, the lower its value (A is less than B)

The special operators perform a variety of functions in a FRED program. Refer to figure 9.3 for information on this group of operators.

Type	Symbol	Definition
Arithmetic	+	Addition
	-	Subtraction
	*	Multiplication
	/	Division
	∧	Exponentiation
String	&	Ampersand — combines text strings
Relational	>	Greater than
	<	Less than
	=	Equal to
	>=	Greater than or equal to
	<=	Less than or equal to
	<>	Not equal
Special	%	Percent — equivalent to division by 100
	()	Groups parameters and expressions
	;	Begins a comment
	,	Separates parameters and expressions
	.	Separates references
	:	Separates beginning and end of region
	"	Delimits beginning and end of string
	[]	Delimits a reference
	{}	Delimits a key

Figure 9.3. FRED operators

PROGRAMMING WITH FRAMES

As we mentioned earlier, a FRED program is entered as a formula so it can exist in any frame type. A FRED program can range from single line programs used to link up frames to sophisticated menu driven systems. While the FRED language is extremely powerful, it is unique in its flexibility. Every Framework user should be able to use the FRED language no matter how simple or advanced their application.

To illustrate FRED, we will develop an example which consolidates information from other frames. Suppose our business had three product lines: gadgets, gizmos and widgets. For each individual product, a financial report is maintained (see figure 9.4).

[GADGETS]

GADGETS:	JANUARY	FEBUARY	MARCH	1ST QTR
SALES	4673.39	4789.03	4573.77	14036.19
COGS:				
LABOR	973.46	1092.12	894.02	2959.60
MATERIALS	1987.23	2304.21	1978.54	6269.98
OVERHEAD	640.56	831.09	597.34	2068.99
TTL COGS	3601.25	4227.42	3469.90	11298.57
INCOME	1072.14	561.61	1103.87	2737.62

[GIZMOS]

GIZMOS:	JANUARY	FEBUARY	MARCH	1ST QTR
SALES	3290.73	3562.91	3347.89	10201.53
COGS:				
LABOR	617.86	653.27	522.78	1793.91
MATERIALS	1753.99	1842.47	1857.41	5453.87
OVERHEAD	529.43	546.04	470.15	1545.62
TTL COGS	2901.28	3041.78	2850.34	8793.40
INCOME	389.45	521.13	497.55	1408.13

Continued on next page

Figure 9.4. Financial report spreadsheets

```
[WIDGETS]

 WIDGETS:   JANUARY   FEBUARY   MARCH     1ST QTR
 SALES      8796.90   9056.87   9879.23     27733
 COGS:
 LABOR      1217.86   1353.27   1522.78   4093.91
 MATERIALS 4353.99   4742.47   4957.41  14053.87
 OVERHEAD  1429.43   1546.04   1609.15   4584.62


 TTL COGS  7001.28   7641.78   8089.34  22732.40

 INCOME    1795.62   1415.09   1789.89   5000.60
```

Figure 9.4. (cont.)   Financial report spreadsheets

If the need exists for another report which consolidates the three reports, the FRED language can be used to create a consolidated report based on the values from the three existing reports.

Figure 9.5 shows the formulas which are used to create the consolidating report.

```
CONSOLIDATED.B1:
   @LIST(GADGETS.B1)

CONSOLIDATED.C1:
   @LIST(GADGETS.C1)

CONSOLIDATED.D1:
   @LIST(GADGETS.D1)

CONSOLIDATED.E1:
   @LIST(GADGETS.E1)

CONSOLIDATED.A2:
   @LIST(GADGETS.A2)

CONSOLIDATED.B2:
   @SUM(GADGETS.B2,GIZMOS.B2,WIDGETS.B2)

CONSOLIDATED.C2:
   @SUM(GADGETS.C2,GIZMOS.C2,WIDGETS.C2)

CONSOLIDATED.D2:
   @SUM(GADGETS.D2,GIZMOS.D2,WIDGETS.D2)

CONSOLIDATED.E2:
   @SUM(GADGETS.E2,GIZMOS.E2,WIDGETS.E2)

CONSOLIDATED.A3:
   @LIST(GADGETS.A3)

CONSOLIDATED.A4:
   @LIST(GADGETS.A4)

CONSOLIDATED.B4:
   @SUM(GADGETS.B4,GIZMOS.B4,WIDGETS.B4)

CONSOLIDATED.C4:
   @SUM(GADGETS.C4,GIZMOS.C4,WIDGETS.C4)

CONSOLIDATED.D4:
   @SUM(GADGETS.D4,GIZMOS.D4,WIDGETS.D4)

CONSOLIDATED.E4:
   @SUM(GADGETS.E4,GIZMOS.E4,WIDGETS.E4)
```

program continued on next page

Figure 9.5. FRED program to consolidate financial reports

```
CONSOLIDATED.A5:
    @LIST(GADGETS.A5)

CONSOLIDATED.B5:
    @SUM(GADGETS.B5,GIZMOS.B5,WIDGETS.B5)

CONSOLIDATED.C5:
    @SUM(GADGETS.C5,GIZMOS.C5,WIDGETS.C5)

CONSOLIDATED.D5:
    @SUM(GADGETS.D5,GIZMOS.D5,WIDGETS.D5)

CONSOLIDATED.E5:
    @SUM(GADGETS.E5,GIZMOS.E5,WIDGETS.E5)

CONSOLIDATED.A6:
    @LIST(GADGETS.A6)

CONSOLIDATED.B6:
    @SUM(GADGETS.B6,GIZMOS.B6,WIDGETS.B6)

CONSOLIDATED.C6:
    @SUM(GADGETS.C6,GIZMOS.C6,WIDGETS.C6)

CONSOLIDATED.D6:
    @SUM(GADGETS.D6,GIZMOS.D6,WIDGETS.D6)

CONSOLIDATED.E6:
    @SUM(GADGETS.E6,GIZMOS.E6,WIDGETS.E6)

CONSOLIDATED.A8:
    @LIST(GADGETS.A8)

CONSOLIDATED.B8:
    @SUM(GADGETS.B8,GIZMOS.B8,WIDGETS.B8)

CONSOLIDATED.C8:
    @SUM(GADGETS.C8,GIZMOS.C8,WIDGETS.C8)

CONSOLIDATED.D8:
    @SUM(GADGETS.D8,GIZMOS.D8,WIDGETS.D8)

CONSOLIDATED.E8:
    @SUM(GADGETS.E8,GIZMOS.E8,WIDGETS.E8)
```

program continued on next page

Figure 9.5. (cont.)   FRED program to consolidate financial
reports

CONSOLIDATED.A10:
@LIST(GADGETS.A10)

CONSOLIDATED.B10:
@SUM(GADGETS.B10,GIZMOS.B10,WIDGETS.B10)

CONSOLIDATED.C10:
@SUM(GADGETS.C10,GIZMOS.C10,WIDGETS.C10)

CONSOLIDATED.D10:
@SUM(GADGETS.D10,GIZMOS.D10,WIDGETS.D10)

CONSOLIDATED.E10:
@SUM(GADGETS.E10,GIZMOS.E10,WIDGETS.E10)

Figure 9.5. (cont.) FRED program to consolidate financial reports

Although the program appears cumbersome, it can be entered by typing in the formulas in cells B1 and B2 and then copying the remainder of the program from these two cells.

When entering a FRED program which references other frames, the frames to be referenced must be loaded onto the desktop. To recalculate a FRED program, the referenced frames must again be loaded onto the desktop.

```
┌[CONSOLIDATED]═══════════════════════════════

  TOTAL:      JANUARY   FEBUARY   MARCH     1ST QTR
  SALES       16761.02  17408.81  17800.89  51970.72
  COGS:
  LABOR        2809.18   3098.66   2939.58   8847.42
  MATERIALS   8095.21    8889.15   8793.36  25777.72
  OVERHEAD    2599.42    2923.17   2676.64   8199.23

  TTL COGS   13503.81   14910.98  14409.58  42824.37

  INCOME      3257.21    2497.83   3391.31   9146.35

```

Figure 9.6. Consolidated financial report

User Defined Functions

Although every spreadsheet which you create is actually programming, the FRED language allows you to add routines to a spreadsheet which in a traditional sense are considered advanced programming. USER DEFINED FUNCTIONS are programming tools which allow you to create and structure program routines.

THE @ OPERATOR

The @ operator will work with your own references just as it does with the built-in FRED functions. You can call a FRED program just as you locate a value using the @ operator. However, the @ operator causes control of Framework to be passed to the referenced frame, spreadsheet cell or variable. The FRED formulas are executed until the referenced program issues an @return or @result or the last expression is executed. Control is then returned to the point where the user function call was initiated. The value generated by the user function is available for use in the frame from which the user function was called. In effect, the USER DEFINED FUNC-TION is executed just as the built-in Framework functions.

Local Variables

In the FRED language, variables may be defined within a program and either text or numeric data may be stored within these variables. The term local signifies that the variable and the data it contains is available only within the FRED program in which it was declared.

A local variable is declared with the @local function. The following formula declares the local variables SALES, COGS and INCOME.

@local(SALES, COGS, INCOME)

The @set function stores data to a local variable. Simply name the variable, followed by a comma, and the data to be assigned to the variable.

@set (SALES, 150000)
@set (COGS, 125000)

The expression which establishes the value of the variable can consist of references to other variables as well.

@set (INCOME, SALES-COGS)

The value of the variable can be returned using the @return function.

@return (INCOME)

The value of the INCOME variable, 25,000, will be returned by this formula.

Local variables should be used as temporary storage for values used in a particular FRED program. Other FRED programs will not have access to the information stored in the local variables. For information which must be shared between FRED programs, frames should be used to establish what is commonly referred to as global variables.

Passing Parameters

User defined functions can accept input parameters known as ITEMS. The parameters are specified when the user defined function is called.

@function name (item1, item2, etc.)

Up to sixteen parameters may be passed. They are numbered beginning with one. The user defined function can then manipulate or use the parameters by referencing the parameters with the @ operator as follows:

@item#

The function @itemcount will specify the number of parameters or items received by the user function.

Menu Generation

A popular approach to organizing programs is through menus. Framework itself is an example of a menu-driven program. Various actions are grouped into submenus. For example, the "Disk" submenu allows the user to store and retrieve disk files.

The FRED language harnesses Framework's outlining capabilities to produce a menu structure. In a Framework outline, the headings and subheadings parallel a menu structure of menus and associated submenus. The @menu function creates a menu system based on the hierarchy of the specified outline.

The @menu function can generate either full screen or bottom screen menus. The full screen menu will appear in the middle of the screen, while the bottom screen menu will list the menu options across the bottom of the screen, leaving the desktop visible.

The menus function much like the Framework menus. The menu options may be invoked using either their first letter or the RETURN key when the option is highlighted.

Keyboard Macros

There are fourty-six Alt-key combinations to which a series of keystrokes can be assigned. Any Framework command or typeable character may be assigned to the Alt-A through Alt-Z, Alt-1 through Alt-0, and Alt-F1 through Alt-F10 keys.

The @performkeys function is used to create a keyboard macro. The series of keyboard entries are entered as a text string. When the macro is called by the appropriate Alt-key, the text string is executed just as if the entries were typed at the keyboard.

The @setmacro function is used to assign one of the forty-six Alt-keys to a macro. The Alt-key is specified, followed by a comma and a reference to the frame where the macro is located.

Appendix A.
FRED Language Functions

Control Functions

@execute	Put a formula in a frame and execute
@getenv	Retrieve an environmental variable
@getformula	Retrieve a formula from source
@list	Group expressions as a single unit
@memavail	"RAM" memory available
@printreturn	Exit from printing operation
@result	Returns the value of a formula
@run	Execute an external program from disk
@select	Execute an expression from a list of expressions
@set	Assign a value to a variable or frame
@setdirectory	Returns current default directory and optionally resets the default directory
@setdrive	Returns current default drive and optionally resets the default drive
@setformula	Replaces formula in the referenced frame
@trace	Record the execution of FRED programs
@while	Loop programming command
@writetextfile	Creates a DOS text file

Date and Time Functions

@date	Enters operating system's date
@date1	Display date as mmm dd, yyy
@date2	Display date as mmm yyy
@date3	Display date as mmm dd
@date4	Display date as Month dd, yyy
@datetime	Returns the specified date and time
@diffdate	Number of days between two dates
@sumdate	Add or subtract days to/from specified date
@time	Enters operating system's time
@time1	Display time as hh:mm (pm/am)
@time2	Display time as hh:mm
@time3	Display time as hh:mm:ss.hh
@today	Reads operating system's date and time

dBASE File Loading Function

@dbasefilter	Filter dBASE file and place onto desktop

Financial Functions

@fv	Future value
@irr	Internal rate of return
@mirr	Modified internal rate of return
@npv	Net present value
@pmt	Payment
@pv	Present value

Function Building Functions

@item	Passes parameter values
@itemcount	Returns number of parameters passed
@local	Defines a local variable
@return	Returns from formula with its value

Graphing Functions

@draw	Draw a picture
@drawgraph	Draw a graph

Logical Functions

@and	Check that all conditions are met
@if	Selects one of two results based on a condition(s)
@isna	Check if parameter is not available
@iserr	Check if parameter is in error
@isabend	Check if there is an abnormal end
@isalpha	Check if parameter is alphabetic
@isnumeric	Check if parameter is numeric
@not	Check if condition is not met
@or	Check whether any of a set of conditions is met

Macro Functions

@echo	Displays keystrokes on the screen
@key	Returns the value of last keypress
@keyfilter	Filters keystrokes
@keyname	Converts a keyname into a text expression
@nextkey	Waits for next keypress and retrieves its value
@performkeys	Produces keystrokes
@setmacro	Assigns a macro key to a frame
@setselection	Navigates to a frame

Numeric Functions

@abs	Absolute value
@acos	Arc cosine
@asin	Arc sine
@atan	Arc tangent
@atan2	"4 Quadrant" Arc tangent
@ceiling	Round up
@cos	Cosine
@exp	Raise e to a power
@floor	Round down
@int	Integer truncation
@ln	Natural logarithm
@log	Logarithm (base 10)
@mod	Modulus
@pi	Pi
@rand	Random number
@round	Round off
@sign	Sign
@sin	Sine
@sqrt	Square root
@tan	Tangent

Printing Functions

@bm	Bottom margin
@ll	Line length
@pl	Page length
@po	Page offset
@pr	Group print functions
@print	Print frame
@st	Set up printer
@tm	Top margin

Footers

@fc	Footer center
@fl	Footer left
@fp	Footer position
@fr	Footer right
@hf	Header/footer start

Headers

@hc	Header center
@hf	Header/Footer start
@hl	Header left
@hp	Header position
@hr	Header right

Ling Spacing

@sk	Skip lines
@sp	Spacing control

Pagination

@kp	Keep on same page
@np	New page
@pn	Page number

Region Walking Functions

@choose	Choose item from a list
@fill	Fill cells or fields with values
@get	Returns value of the current element in a region
@hlookup	Lookup value in a horizontal table
@next	Return value after the current element in a region
@put	Places a value in the current element
@reset	Makes current element the first element of a region
@vlookup	Lookup in a vertical table

Sound Generation Function

@beep	Produces a tone from a speaker

Statistical Functions

@avg	Average
@count	Counts numeric items
@max	Maximum value
@min	Minimum value
@std	Standard deviation
@sum	Sum
@var	Variance

String Functions

@business	Converts a numeric value to text in business format
@chr	Converts number into character
@currency	Converts a numeric value to text in currency format
@decimal	Converts a numeric value to text in decimal format
@integer	Converts a numeric value to text in integer format
@len	Length of parameter
@mid	Extract portion of parameter

@rept	Repeats an expression
@scientific	Converts a numeric value to text in scientific format
@textselection	Returns a currently selected text
@value	Converts text to a numeric value

Tailoring Functions

@dollar	Display numeric values in dollar format
@milli	Display numeric values in milli format
@nationalize	Standardize currency unit for a frame
@pound	Display numeric values in pound format
@thousands	Display numeric values in thousands format
@unit	Define new unit for numbers formatted as currency
@yen	Display numeric values in yen format

User Interface Functions

@display	Display the specified frame
@eraseprompt	Erase message area on bottom of screen
@inputline	Prompts user for input
@menu	Presents specified frame as a series of menus
@prompt	Display prompt on bottom line of screen in message area
@quitmenu	Exit from a menu system

Appendix B.
ASCII Codes

In the following table the ASCII codes (in decimal) are listed with their associated characters. These characters can be generated by pressing the Alt key, entering the ASCII decimal codes via the numeric keypad, and releasing the Alt key.

ASCII Value*	Character	ASCII Value	Character
000	(null)	016	►
001	☺	017	◄
002	●	018	↕
003	♥	019	‼
004	♦	020	π
005	♣	021	₴
006	♠	022	▬
007	♦	023	↕
008	■	024	↑
009	(tab)	025	↓
010	◘	026	→
011	♂	027	←
012	♀	028	∟
013	(carriage return)	029	↔
014	♫	030	▲
015	☼	031	▼

* Decimal

225

ASCII Value	Character	ASCII Value	Character	ASCII Value	Character
032	(space)	071	G	110	n
033	!	072	H	111	o
034	"	073	I	112	p
035	#	074	J	113	q
036	$	075	K	114	r
037	%	076	L	115	s
038	&	077	M	116	t
039	'	078	N	117	u
040	(	079	O	118	v
041	)	080	P	119	w
042	*	081	Q	120	x
043	+	082	R	121	y
044	,	083	S	122	z
045	−	084	T	123	{
046	.	085	U	124	|
047	/	086	V	125	}
048	0	087	W	126	~
049	1	088	X	127	△
050	2	089	Y	128	Ç
051	3	090	Z	129	ü
052	4	091	[	130	é
053	5	092	\	131	â
054	6	093	]	132	ä
055	7	094	^	133	à
056	8	095	—	134	å
057	9	096	`	135	ç
058	:	097	a	136	ê
059	;	098	b	137	ë
060	<	099	c	138	è
061	=	100	d	139	ï
062	>	101	e	140	î
063	?	102	f	141	ì
064	@	103	g	142	Ä
065	A	104	h	143	Å
066	B	105	i	144	É
067	C	106	j	145	æ
068	D	107	k	146	Æ
069	E	108	l	147	ô
070	F	109	m	148	ö

ASCII Value	Character	ASCII Value	Character	ASCII Value	Character
149	ò	188	⌐	227	π
150	û	189	⌐	228	Σ
151	ù	190	⌐	229	o
152	ÿ	191	┐	230	μ
153	Ö	192	└	231	τ
154	Ü	193	┴	232	Φ
155	¢	194	┬	233	Θ
156	£	195	├	234	Ω
157	¥	196	—	235	δ
158	Pt	197	┼	236	∞
159	f	198	╞	237	$\varnothing$
160	á	199	╟	238	ϵ
161	í	200	╚	239	$\cap$
162	ó	201	╔	240	$\equiv$
163	ú	202	╩	241	$\pm$
164	ñ	203	╦	242	$\geq$
165	Ñ	204	╠	243	$\leq$
166	a	205	═	244	$\lceil$
167	o	206	╬	245	$\rfloor$
168	¿	207	╧	246	$\div$
169	⌐	208	╨	247	$\approx$
170	¬	209	╤	248	$\circ$
171	½	210	╥	249	$\bullet$
172	¼	211	╙	250	$\cdot$
173	¡	212	╘	251	$\sqrt{}$
174	≪	213	╒	252	n
175	≫	214	╓	253	^{2}
176	▒	215	╫	254	■
177	▓	216	╪	255	(blank 'FF')
178	▓	217	┘		
179	│	218	┌		
180	┤	219	█		
181	╡	220	▄		
182	╢	221	▌		
183	╖	222	▐		
184	╕	223	▀		
185	╣	224	$\propto$		
186	║	225	β		
187	╗	226	Γ		

Appendix C.
Menu Command Reference Guide

DISK Menu

Shortcut	Command	Description
∧ DG	Get file by name	Retrieves a file.
∧ DS	Save and continue	Saves document and allows you to continue processing.
∧ DP	Put away	Saves document and clears it from desktop.
∧ DC	Clean up desktop	Closes all frames on desktop.
∧ DW	Write DOS text file	Allows a document to be saved on disk as a DOS text file.
∧ DD	DOS access	Allows you to access DOS within Framework.
∧ DU	Utilities	Runs the desktop program UTIL.
∧ DT	Telecommunications	Accesses telecommunications submenu.
∧ DQ	Quit Framework	Exits Framework.

CREATE Menu

Shortcut	Command	Description
^CO	Outline	Create outline frame.
^CE	Empty/Word Frame	Create empty word frame.
^CS	Spreadsheet	Create spreadsheet frame.
^CD	Database	Create database frame.
^CW	Width (# Cols/Fields)	Specifies width of spreadsheet or data base frame.
^CH	Height (#Rows/Records)	Specifies height of spreadsheet or data base frame.
^CC	Columns/Fields Add	Inserts columns in a spreadsheet or data base.
^CR	Rows/Records: Add	inserts rows in a spreadsheet or data base.

EDIT Menu

Shortcut	Command	Description
^EU	Undo	Reverses most recent action.
^EC	Columns/Fields: Remove	Deletes columns from the data base or spreadsheet.
^ER	Rows/Records: Remove	Deletes rows from the data base or spreadsheet.
^EL	Lock first column/row	Prevents the first row and column of a spreadsheet or data base from being scrolled off the screen.
^EP	Protect from editing	Prevents data from being inadvertently edited or erased.
^EA	Allow Editing	Allows editing.
^ET	Typeover	Characters entered replace or typeover existing characters.
^ED	Display hidden characters	Causes characters not generally displayed to appear.

LOCATE Menu

Shortcut	Command	Description
^ LA	Ascending sort	Specifies the sort direction as ascending.
^ LD	Descending sort	Specifies the sort direction as descending.
^ LS	Search	Finds specified characters in a document.
^ LR	Replace	Finds specified characters in a document and replaces these with a new set of characters.
^ LL	Labels included	Determines whether or not frame labels will be included in the Search or Replace.
^ LC	Contents included	Determines whether or not frame contents will be included in the Search or Replace.
^ LF	Formulas included	Determines whether or not formulas will be included in the Search or Replace.
^ LI	Ignore capitalization	Determines whether or not capital letters will be regarded in a different manner than their lower case counterparts.

FRAMES Menu

Shortcut	Command	Description
^ FO	Open all	Opens all frames within the selected frame. Often used to restore data base records hidden by filtering.
^ FC	Close all	Closes all frames within the selected frame.

Continued on next page

Shortcut	Command	Description
∧ FS	Size all	Results in all column arranged frames within the selected frame being adjusted to the size of the enclosing frame.
∧ FB	Blank All	Blanks unprotected data in the selected frame.
∧ FP	Put in column	Places frames at the same level as the selected frame in a column along the left side of the enclosing frame.
∧ FA	Allow free dragging	Enables vertical as well as horizontal dragging.
∧ FV	View page numbers	Page numbers can only be displayed for frames in the outline view. When on, this command identifies the page number at which each selected frame and their sub-frames will begin when printed.
∧ FN	Number labels	Displays outline level numbers for all selected frames and their subframes.
∧ FR	Reveal type	Displays a letter as follows after the frame label to indicate the type of frame: D=Data base frame E=Empty frame G=Graph frame S=Spreadsheet frame W=Word frame
∧ FD	Display labels	Determines whether or not the frame label is displayed.
∧ FH	Hide borders	Hides the border lines and frame labels of the selected frame and all subframes.

WORDS Menu

Shortcut	Command	Description
∧WN	Normal	Display text in normal style. Eliminates bold, italic, and underline styling.
∧WB	Bold	Selected text is displayed and printed in bold.
∧WU	Underline	Selected text is underlined.
∧WI	Italic	Selected text is italicized.
∧WA	Align left	Lines are aligned with the left margin. The right margin is ragged.
∧WF	Flush right	Lines are aligned with the right margin. The left margin is ragged.
∧WJ	Justify	Spaces are inserted in the text so that both margins are justified.
∧WC	Center	Lines are centered between the left and right margins.
∧WL	Left margin	Indicates position for the left margin.
∧WR	Right margin	Indicates position for the right margin.
∧WP	Paragraph indent	Specifies the number of positions indented for a new paragraph.
∧WT	Tab size	Specifies the number of positions for a tab.

NUMBERS Menu

Shortcut	Command	Description
∧ND	Decimal places	Indicates the number of decimal places displayed for the current cell. The original number can be seen in the status panel.

Continued on next page

Shortcut	Command	Description
^NG	General (number)	Indicates the default number style (2 decimal places).
^NI	Integer	Displays current cell value in integer format.
^NF	Fixed decimal	Displays current cell value in fixed decimal format.
^NC	Currency	Displays current cell data as a dollar value.
^NB	Business	Displays current cell data in the same format as Currency without the $ sign.
^NP	Percent	Displays current cell data as a percent value.
^NS	Scientific	Displays data in exponential notation.
^NW	Words Left/#s Right	Words are aligned with the cell's left margin; numbers with the right.
^NL	Left	Words and numbers are aligned to the left.
^NR	Right	Words and numbers are aligned to the right.
^NM	Middle	Words and numbers are centered within the cell or field.
^NOA	Automatic	Formulas are automatically calculated when they are entered or edited.
^NOM	Manual	Formulas are recalculated only if F5 is pressed.
^NOR	Row-wise	The spreadsheet is recalculated row by row, from top to bottom.
^NON	Natural	Recalculates cells in the order indicated by their relationships.

GRAPHS Menu

Shortcut	Command	Description
^ GD	Draw new graph	Draws the new graph.
^ GA	Add to existing graph	Adds an overlay to an existing graph.
^ GB	Bar graph	Draw a bar graph.
^ GS	Stacked bar graph	Draw a stacked bar graph.
^ GP	Pie graph	Draw a pie graph.
^ GL	Line graph	Draw a line.
^ GM	Marked points graph	Draw a marked points graph.
^ GX	X-Y graphs	Draw an X-Y graph.
^ GC	Column has X-axis labels	The column headings are used for X-axis labels.
^ GR	Row has X-axis labels	The row headings are used for X-axis labels.
^ GOX	X-axis title	Allows specification of X-axis title.
^ GOY	Y-axis title	Allows specification of Y-axis title.
^ GOM	Manual Y-axis scaling	Allows the scale and the range of the Y-axis to be specified.
^ GOL	Lowest Y-axis value	Indicates minimum Y-axis value.
^ GOH	Highest Y-axis value	Indicates maximum Y-axis value.
^ GOS	Scale in increments of	Allows specification of scale settings.
^ GOE	Explode pie slice	The indicated pie graph slice will be offset.

PRINT Menu

Shortcut	Command	Description
^ PB	Begin	Starts printing.
^ PS	Stop	Ends printing
^ PP	Pause	Temporarily ends printing.
^ PW	Wait	When on, waits until a key is pressed before subsequent frames are printed.
^ PDF	First Printer	Specifies output to the first printer.
^ PDS	Second Printer	Specifies output to the second printer.
^ PDP	Plotter	Specifies output to the plotter.
^ PDD	DOS text file	Saves formatted document as a DOS text file.
^ POB	Begin on page	Select beginning page number.
^ POE	End on page	Select ending page number.
^ PON	Number of copies	Specifies the number of printed copies.
^ POS	Skip closed frames	Closed frames are not printed.
^ POF	Formulas only	Print formulas only.
^ POP	Print frame labels	Frame labels are printed.

Appendix D.
Framework Error Messages

An error message is displayed whenever the operator begins an action that would destroy data, enters a formula with a syntax error, or attempts an action which cannot be performed.

Most of these error messages are self-explanatory. The meanings of the following error messages are not self-evident.

Error Message	Description
#DIV/0!	Division by zero is not allowed.
#N/A!	The referenced frame is not available. This error generally occurs because no data or formulas had been entered.
#NAME?	FRED is unable to locate the referenced frame.
#NULL	Often occurs when a FRED formula references a parameter whose value was not passed.
#NUM!	A function was used in an illegal manner or an expression evaluated to a value that was either too large or too small.
#REF!	The referenced value cannot be located. This is often due to the deletion of the referenced frame, a change in the name of the referenced frame, or a misspelling of the reference.
#VALUE	String, numeric and logical values have been used improperly resulting in an incorrect referenced value in the formula.

Appendix E.
Framework Utilities

Framework's Utilities disk includes a number of valuable utility programs that can perform a wide range of functions, from translating Wordstar files to formatting and checking diskettes. The Utilities disk also includes printer driver files, screen driver files, and the telecommunications driver, example and help files.

Observe the following steps to select a utility program:

1. Insert the Utility disk in a disk drive, select the corresponding drive indicator on the desktop and press [RET]. The Utility programs will be displayed in the drive's frame.

2. Press [DOWNLEVEL] to move into the frame body. Select the desired file and press [RET].

The exception is the 1-2-3 conversion program which is loaded from DOS rather than Framework.

The Utilities disk's -README.FW file contains a description of these various utilities. You can examine -README.FW by bringing it onto the desktop. The following is displayed within -README.FW's frame:

1 Introduction — (Press F9 and/or F10 to read more)
2 DiskUtil   — perform disk maintenance from within Framework
3 LIB   — an example of Framework Function Libraries
4 Maclib   — standard Framework macros
5 MailUtil   — customized form letters and mailing labels
6 Converting Wordstar "Document" Files
7 Converting Visicalc DIF Files
8 Converting Lotus 123 Spreadsheets
9 A Word About Printer Drivers
10 How to print this document

You can obtain a detailed description of each utility program by selecting the corresponding choice from the -README.FW frame and pressing F9. Press F9 again to return to the frame.

For your convenience, we'll briefly describe the utilities in the following sections. One final note, however, many of the utilities must be recalculated using F5 prior to their use.

DiskUtil

DiskUtil must be recalculated when it is loaded by pressing F5 with the highlight on the frame border. Press Alt-D to access the utility. Then select the desired operation from the menu at the bottom of the screen:

> **Save Defaults** — allows you to set new DiskUtil defaults and save these. The current defaults assume a dual floppy drive system.
>
> **Format Disk** — formats a diskette.
>
> **Check Disk** — returns the available free disk space and available RAM.
>
> **Disk Copy** — copies one diskette's contents to another. The newly copied diskette is automatically formatted.
>
> **Make Directory** — creates a subdirectory.

LIB

LIB is an area used to store user-defined functions. These may later be called by FRED programs.

Maclib

This file contains a number of useful macros including:

RECORD — connects a series of keystrokes to an Alt key combination.

GO TO — ask for a frame name. If the frame is found, the program proceeds to it.

GO BACK — returns to location prior to the last GO TO.

CUT — stores text presently selected for later use by PASTE.

PASTE — accesses text stored by CUT.

SPLIT FRAME INTO TWO — creates a new frame after the cursor position.

MailUtil

This is a FRED program that allows you to easily output form letters. One document is used as the master. Information from data base fields is then inserted into this master to customize individual variations.

Wordstar Conversion Program

WS2.FW allows easy conversion of Wordstar files into Framework desktop files.

DIF Conversion Program

TRANSDIF.FW allows DIF files to be converted into Framework spreadsheet frames.

1-2-3 Conversion Program

TRANS123.EXE converts Lotus 1-2-3 .wks files into Framework spreadsheet frames.

Index

243

ABOUT THE
WEBER SYSTEMS, INC. STAFF

In 1982, Weber Systems, Inc. began a start-up publishing division specializing in books related to the personal computer field. They initially published three books, and within a year, expanded their list to eighteen machine-specific titles, with fourteen more scheduled for early 1984.

All Weber Systems USER'S HANDBOOKS are created by an in-house editorial staff with extensive backgrounds in computer science and technical writing. The three basic tenets of their publishing philosophy are: quality, timeliness and maintenance (frequent updating).

Weber Systems is located in Cleveland, Ohio.

CENTURY COMMUNICATIONS

A range of useful computer books for both business and home users are available from Century Communications. Please write for up-to-date catalogue and stocklist.

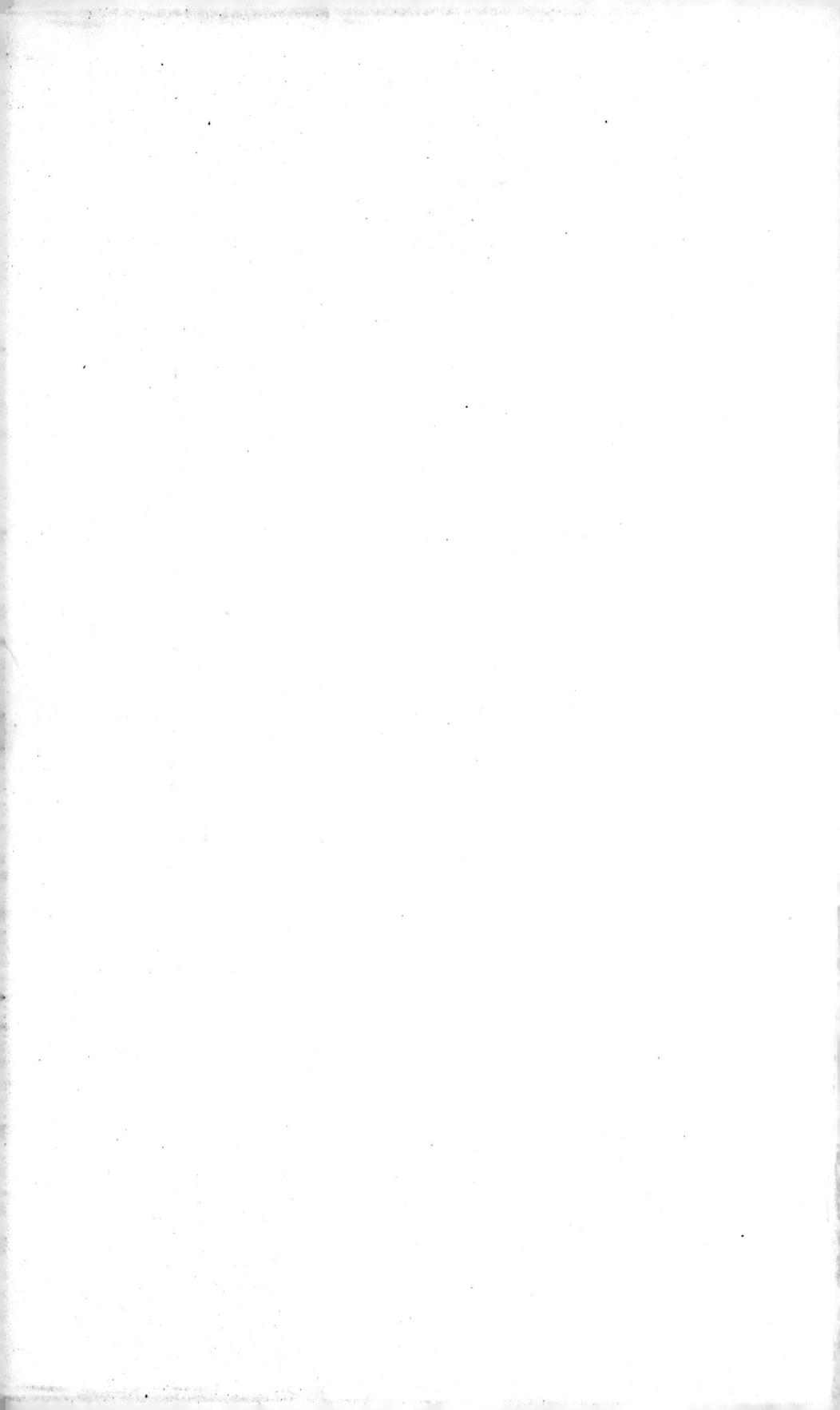